P9-BZJ-306

the flavors of

Restaurant LuLu

The Flavors of Restaurant LuLu
Copyright 2006 by Restaurant LuLu, Inc.
All rights reserved.
No portion of this book may be reproduced or utilized in any form or by any electronic, mechanical, or other means without prior written permission of the publisher, Restaurant LuLu, Inc.
Printed in Hong Kong.

First Edition

Printed on acid-free paper

Library of Congress Control Number: 2005910287

Restaurant LuLu, Inc.
1245 Folsom St.
San Francisco, CA 94103
888-693-5800 / 415-255-8686
customerservice@restaurantlulu.com
http://www.restaurantlulu.com

ISBN-13: 978-0-9774901-0-3
ISBN-10: 0-9774901-0-6

To everyone at Restaurant LuLu, Zibibbo, Azie and LuLu Petite without whose time, effort and encouragement this book could not have happened.

To our customers, whose love of life and good food continues to inspire us year after year.

Contents

Introduction

On New Year's Eve 1992, we opened our doors to celebrate not only the new year, but the beginning of a new venture called Restaurant LuLu. Located in the then fledgling neighborhood of SoMa (south of Market Street) in San Francisco, customers were drawn by the glow of the wood-burning rotisserie and the wonderful aromas of the rustic cuisine that integrated the flavors of Provence with California ingredients.

Restaurant LuLu has been a popular destination for both visitors and locals ever since that fateful night. A fun place to dine and drink, the restaurant has received many honors throughout the years, including being selected by *The San Francisco Chronicle* as one of its 2005 Top 100 Bay Area Restaurants and receiving *Wine Spectator* magazine's "Best of Award of Excellence" for 2004 and 2005.

Our family has grown to include three additional restaurants in California, Azie in San Francisco , Zibibbo in Palo Alto, and a second Restaurant LuLu in Mammoth Lakes, four gourmet delicatessens named LuLu Petite, and a catering company. Although the menus at each establishment reflect the influences of different worldwide cuisines, the mission of each is the same – to create distinctive dishes with bold flavors using the freshest ingredients.

In 1997 our chefs decided to bottle some of the unique condiments they'd created at the restaurant and launched Restaurant LuLu Gourmet Products. From those initial offerings, which included Fig Balsamic Vinegar and White Truffle Honey, the LuLu line has grown to over 50 products including sauces, vinegars, vinaigrettes, tapenades, marinades, seasonings, and sweets that truly capture the essence of the LuLu dining experience. Over the years the products have won many awards and have received recognition from publications including *Gourmet*, *Food & Wine*, and *Sunset* magazines.

LuLu products are perhaps best known for their unique flavor combinations, and we are constantly asked for new and fun ways to cook with them at home. In these pages our chefs have assembled some of their best recipes for your enjoyment. We hope they inspire you to explore all of the flavors of Restaurant LuLu.

Antipasti

Bruschetta with Grilled Figs, Prosciutto and Pierre Robert Cheese

4 to 6 servings

Featuring: **LuLu Lavender Honey Grilling Sauce**
LuLu White Truffle Honey

Ingredients: 1 loaf ciabatta bread (or levain or other rustic, country bread)
2 tablespoons extra virgin olive oil
salt and pepper to taste
10 figs, ends trimmed and cut in half
1/4 cup LuLu Lavender Honey Grilling Sauce
1/4 pound prosciutto, thinly sliced
1/2 pound Pierre Robert cheese or other creamy soft-ripened cheese
1/4 cup LuLu White Truffle Honey
minced chives for garnish if desired

Preparation: Heat grill to medium-high heat.

Cut bread into 1/2-inch thick slices, drizzle both sides with olive oil and sprinkle with salt and pepper. Grill bread slices for about 2 minutes on each side until bread is golden brown. Arrange bread slices in one layer on an ovenproof serving platter.

In a small bowl, toss figs with LuLu Lavender Honey Grilling Sauce. Remove figs from Grilling Sauce and leave excess Grilling Sauce in bowl. Grill figs cut-side down for about 1-1/2 minutes, and return hot figs to bowl with excess Grilling Sauce. When figs are cool enough to handle, remove them from the Grilling Sauce, reserve excess Sauce again, and cut each fig half in half again yielding one-quarter pieces. Set aside.

Preheat oven to 400°

Cut prosciutto slices into 1-inch wide strips and toss in bowl with reserved Grilling Sauce. Place bread slices in a single layer on an ovenproof platter. Arrange prosciutto over bread slices and top with fig pieces. Cut cheese into thin slices or wedges and place atop figs.

continued

Place platter into oven for 1 minute until cheese is lightly melted. Remove from oven and drizzle LuLu White Truffle Honey over bruschetta. Garnish with chives if desired and serve immediately.

Note:

Pierre Robert is a soft-ripened, triple crème cow's milk cheese with a bloomy rind. This artisanal cheese, with its rich and buttery flavor, comes from Ile-de-France near Paris. If you can't find it, either Saint André, brie or camembert would be good substitutes.

Fava Bean, Red Onion and Parmesan Salad

4 to 6 appetizer servings

Featuring: **LuLu Preserved Meyer Lemon & Artichoke Vinaigrette**
               LuLu Marinated Leeks

Ingredients: 2 cups fresh fava beans, shelled and hulled (see Note)
               1/2 cup thinly sliced red onion (about 1/2 onion)
               1 - 1 ounce piece Parmesan cheese, shaved into thin strips with a
                 vegetable peeler
               2 tablespoons LuLu Preserved Meyer Lemon & Artichoke Vinaigrette
               2 tablespoons LuLu Marinated Leeks
               1 tablespoon fresh chopped thyme
               salt and pepper to taste

Preparation: In a medium bowl, combine fava beans, red onion and half of
               Parmesan cheese. In a separate bowl stir together LuLu Preserved Meyer
               Lemon & Artichoke Vinaigrette, LuLu Marinated Leeks, and thyme. Toss
               fava mixture with vinaigrette mixture, taste and adjust salt and pepper.
               Top with remaining Parmesan cheese and serve.

Note: After shelling fava bean pods, you will see that each individual fava bean has a tough "skin" (called a hull) on it. Remove these hulls by blanching the beans for 4 – 5 minutes, then rinse under cold, running water and squeeze the fava bean out of its hull.

Other LuLu Products: If LuLu Marinated Leeks is not available, substitute LuLu Preserved Meyer Lemon in Olive Oil.

Mustard Roasted Mushrooms

6 to 8 servings

Featuring: **LuLu Mustard & Herbes de Provence Grilling Sauce**
                 LuLu Basil Pistou

Ingredients: 2 pounds mixed fresh specialty mushrooms (see Note)
                 4 bay leaves
                 2 tablespoons extra virgin olive oil
                 2 tablespoons LuLu Mustard & Herbes de Provence Grilling Sauce
                 salt and pepper to taste
                 2 tablespoons LuLu Basil Pistou

Preparation: Preheat oven to 450°

                 Clean mushrooms by either using a mushroom brush, shaking under
                 cold, running water, or wiping off any dirt with a towel. Remove any hard
                 stems and keep small mushrooms whole; halve or quarter any that are
                 large.

                 In a medium bowl, toss mushrooms with bay leaves, olive oil, LuLu
                 Mustard & Herbes de Provence Grilling Sauce, and salt and pepper.
                 Place mushrooms on a baking sheet and roast for 5 minutes. Remove
                 from oven and place mushrooms in a clean bowl.

                 While mushrooms are still hot, stir in LuLu Basil Pistou.

                 To serve: place mushrooms on a platter or individual plates. Serve hot or
                 at room temperature, on its own or as part of an antipasta plate.

Note: All grocery stores offer white cultivated mushrooms, however in recent years specialty mushrooms have become more widely available. With their different shapes and textures, we like the "woodsy" flavor that these add to recipes. Look for varieties such as cèpes, chanterelles, cremini, hen-of-the-woods, morels, portobello, shitake and wood ear.

Other LuLu Products: If LuLu Basil Pistou is not available, substitute LuLu Truffled Artichoke Tapenade.

Parmesan Antipasta

4 appetizer servings

Featuring:	**LuLu Fig Balsamic Vinegar**
	LuLu Fennel, Olive & Onion Confit

Ingredients:

1 - 4 ounce piece Parmesan cheese, preferably Parmigiano-Reggiano, broken into large pieces
2 tablespoons LuLu Fig Balsamic Vinegar
1/2 jar LuLu Fennel, Olive & Onion Confit
2 tablespoons Italian (flat leaf) parsley for garnish
1 baguette

Preparation:

Break Parmesan cheese into small chunks and arrange on serving platter. Drizzle cheese with LuLu Fig Balsamic Vinegar and serve with LuLu Fennel, Olive & Onion Confit on the side. Garnish with whole leaves of Italian parsley and serve with baguette.

Note: To make individual appetizers, slice baguette thinly and top bread with shavings of Parmesan cheese. Drizzle with Lulu Fig Balsamic Vinegar and top with a dollop of LuLu Fennel, Olive & Onion Confit.

Roasted Baby Beets with Currants and Almonds

6 servings

Featuring: **LuLu Preserved Meyer Lemon & Rosemary Marinade**
LuLu Fig & Meyer Lemon Balsamic Vinegar

Ingredients: 4 bunches (about 3 pounds) baby beets in assorted colors
2 tablespoons LuLu Preserved Meyer Lemon & Rosemary Marinade
2 tablespoons extra virgin olive oil
salt to taste
1-1/2 tablespoons plus 1 teaspoon currants
4 tablespoons chopped fresh parsley
2 tablespoons LuLu Fig & Meyer Lemon Balsamic Vinegar
1/3 cup slivered almonds, toasted
1/4 cup chopped arugula for garnish if desired

Preparation: Preheat oven to 400°.

Remove greens from beets and reserve for another use. Gently rinse off beets and place in a roasting pan with 1/4 cup water. Cover pan with foil and roast for 25 minutes, until fork-tender. Remove from oven.

With a slotted spoon, remove beets from roasting pan and place on a towel. Peel beets while still warm by gently rubbing them with a towel.

Cut beets into quarters and place into a bowl. Toss beets with LuLu Preserved Meyer Lemon & Rosemary Marinade and olive oil. Sprinkle with salt, 1-1/2 tablespoons currants, 3 tablespoons parsley and toss to combine. Add LuLu Fig & Meyer Lemon Balsamic Vinegar and almonds and toss again.

To serve: spoon beets onto a platter and sprinkle with remaining 1 teaspoon currants and 1 tablespoon parsley. Top with chopped arugula if desired.

Note: *Beets are root vegetables that are available most of the year. Baby beets are more tender and sweeter than larger ones, however if they are not available, you can substitute large beets by roasting them longer and cutting them into eighths instead of quarters.*

Other LuLu Products: *If LuLu Preserved Meyer Lemon & Rosemary Marinade is not available, substitute LuLu Preserved Meyer Lemon, Fennel & Sage Marinade. If LuLu Fig & Meyer Lemon Balsamic Vinegar is not available, substitute another LuLu Balsamic Vinegar.*

Baked Brie in Phyllo

4 appetizer servings

Featuring: **LuLu Fig Marionberry & Balsamic Jam**
LuLu Herbes de Provence Seasoning

Ingredients: 3 sheets phyllo dough, thawed if frozen
2 tablespoons melted butter
1 small whole wheel of brie, up to 8 ounces
2 tablespoons LuLu Fig Marionberry & Balsamic Jam
1 teaspoon LuLu Herbes de Provence Seasoning
1 baguette, thinly sliced

Preparation: Preheat oven to 350°.

Working quickly to prevent phyllo dough from drying out, lay 1 sheet of phyllo on a large, lightly-buttered baking sheet and brush dough lightly with melted butter. Lay second sheet over it and brush with butter and repeat with third sheet.

Place brie wheel in center of prepared phyllo. Spread LuLu Fig Marionberry & Balsamic Jam over top of brie, and then sprinkle with ½ teaspoon LuLu Herbes de Provence Seasoning.

Encase brie in phyllo by wrapping all 3 sheets of dough around the brie and gathering ends of phyllo at the top center of brie. Do not trim excess phyllo; allow extra phyllo to stand on top of brie.

Bake phyllo-wrapped brie in oven for 8 to 10 minutes, until phyllo is golden brown.

Remove from oven and sprinkle with remaining LuLu Herbes de Provence Seasoning. Serve immediately with sliced baguette.

Note: *Phyllo (also spelled filo) is a paper-thin pastry dough used in Greek and Middle-Eastern baking. It is widely-available frozen, but it's worth looking for fresh dough if possible. To make sure that the dough doesn't dry out while you are working with some of the sheets, be sure to cover remaining sheets with a slightly damp (not wet) kitchen towel.*

Other LuLu Products: *If LuLu Fig Marionberry & Balsamic Jam is not available, substitute another LuLu jam or LuLu Meyer Lemon & Caramelized Onion Marmalade.*

Rabbit Rillettes with Herbes de Provence

4 to 6 appetizer servings

Featuring:
LuLu Mustard with Herbes de Provence
LuLu Herbes de Provence Seasoning
LuLu Meyer Lemon & Caramelized Onion Marmalade

Ingredients:
1 small whole rabbit, cut into quarters, or 4 rabbit legs
3 to 4 cups melted duck fat or olive oil
1 tablespoon LuLu Mustard with Herbes de Provence
1 tablespoon diced shallot
2 teaspoons sherry wine vinegar
1 teaspoon LuLu Herbes de Provence Seasoning
2 teaspoons chopped fresh parsley
3 tablespoons LuLu Meyer Lemon & Caramelized Onion Marmalade
1 baguette, thinly sliced

Preparation:
Preheat oven to 250°.

Arrange rabbit pieces in a deep baking dish or ovenproof saucepan that is just big enough to hold pieces in a single layer. Cover rabbit with melted duck fat or olive oil, place in oven and roast until meat is tender and easily pulls away from the bone, about 3 hours. (Fat should remain at a slow simmer throughout the cooking time.) Remove rabbit from oven, and carefully lift pieces from fat. Allow rabbit and fat to cool separately.

When rabbit is cool enough to handle but still warm, pull meat from bones and shred meat by hand; you should have about 2 cups of rabbit meat. Reserve 3 tablespoons of fat. (Recipe can be prepared up to this point in advance. Cover and refrigerate meat and fat separately until just before serving.)

Preheat oven to 400°.

(If rabbit has been prepared in advance, gently heat meat and fat in separate pans before proceeding.) In a large bowl, gently stir LuLu Mustard with Herbes de Provence, shallot, vinegar and LuLu Herbes de Provence Seasoning into rabbit meat. Stir in reserved cooking fat and then add parsley. Press the mixture into a small casserole or ovenproof skillet. Place in oven and roast for 6 minutes until heated through.

continued

Remove rillettes from oven and top with LuLu Meyer Lemon & Caramelized Onion Marmalade. Serve with sliced baguette.

Note: *Rillettes are a classic French preparation that was originally used as a way to preserve meat and fowl such as duck. The initial roasting requires a long, unattended cooking time; it's easiest to do this part in advance and finish the recipe just before serving.*

Celery Root Salad
with Preserved Lemons and Fresh Herbs

8 servings

Featuring: **LuLu Preserved Meyer Lemon in Olive OIl**
LuLu French Mayonnaise with Dijon Mustard

Ingredients: 2 medium-sized celery roots
salt and pepper to taste
2 tablespoons LuLu Preserved Meyer Lemon in Olive Oil
1/4 cup LuLu French Mayonnaise with Dijon Mustard
juice of 1 lemon
2 tablespoons chopped celery leaves
2 tablespoons chopped fresh parsley or more for garnish if desired
2 tablespoons minced chives or more for garnish if desired
large, whole butter lettuce leaves

Preparation: Trim celery root of leaves and stalk if there are any. Peel celery roots and cut into thin slices, then stack and cut slices into matchstick-thin pieces. (This can also be done with a mandoline.)

Place celery root into a large bowl and sprinkle with salt and pepper to taste. Spoon in LuLu Preserved Meyer Lemon in Olive Oil and LuLu French Mayonnaise with Dijon Mustard and stir to combine. Add lemon juice and toss, then add celery leaves, parsley and chives and toss again.

To serve: line platter or bowl with butter lettuce leaves and spoon salad on top.

| Note: | Celery root is also known as celery knob or celeriac. This salad is ready to serve immediately, but it is even better if it marinates in its dressing for a day or two. |
| Other LuLu Products: | If LuLu Preserved Meyer Lemon in Olive Oil is not available, substitute LuLu Preserved Meyer Lemon & Rosemary Marinade. If LuLu French Mayonnaise with Dijon Mustard is not available, substitute another LuLu Mayonnaise. |

Crostini Antipasti

10 to 12 appetizer servings

Featuring:
LuLu Green Olive Tapenade
LuLu Sun-Dried Tomato & Porcini Tapenade
LuLu Olive Tapenade
LuLu Truffled Artichoke Tapenade
LuLu White Truffle Honey
LuLu Meyer Lemon & Caramelized Onion Marmalade
LuLu Red Plum & Roasted Onion Conserve

Ingredients:
2 1-pound baguettes, preferably day-old
1 cup extra virgin olive oil
2 ounces pecorino pepato, thinly sliced
3 tablespoons LuLu Green Olive Tapenade
2 ounces fresh mozzarella, cut into small pieces
3 tablespoons LuLu Sun-Dried Tomato & Porcini Tapenade
1-1/2 ounces thinly-sliced salami
3 tablespoons LuLu Olive Tapenade
3 ounces fresh goat cheese
3 tablespoons LuLu Truffled Artichoke Tapenade
3 ounces brie or other soft-ripened cheese, cut into small pieces
3 tablespoons LuLu White Truffle Honey
3 ounces country style pork pâté or rabbit rillettes (see page 14)
3 tablespoons LuLu Meyer Lemon & Caramelized Onion Marmalade
1 ounce thinly-sliced prosciutto
3 tablespoons LuLu Red Plum & Roasted Onion Conserve

Preparation:
To make crostini: preheat oven to 325°.

Slice baguettes as thinly as possible. Brush each slice very lightly with olive oil and place slices in a single layer on a large baking sheet. Bake 10 to 15 minutes or until golden brown and crisp. Set aside and allow to cool. (You can prepare crostini in advance and store at room temperature in an airtight container for a few days.)

To assemble: pair the remaining ingredients as follows on the crostini and serve on a decorative platter.

continued

- pecorino pepato topped with a dollop of LuLu Green Olive Tapenade
- fresh mozzarella topped with a dollop of LuLu Sun-Dried Tomato & Porcini Tapenade
- salami topped with a dollop of LuLu Olive Tapenade
- goat cheese topped with a dollop of LuLu Truffled Artichoke Tapenade
- brie topped with a drizzle of LuLu White Truffle Honey
- pâté or rabbit rillettes topped with LuLu Meyer Lemon & Caramelized Onion Marmalade
- prosciutto topped with LuLu Red Plum & Roasted Onion Conserve

Note: *Alternatively, you can serve the crostini and toppings separately and allow your guests to assemble their favorite combinations. All quantities are approximate, so feel free to use more or less as the mood strikes you.*

Small Plates

Crab and Heirloom Tomato Soup

6 servings

Featuring:

LuLu Heirloom Tomato & Roasted Garlic Sauce
LuLu Roasted Tomato Harissa
LuLu Saffron & Garlic Rouille

Ingredients:

1/4 cup extra virgin olive oil
1 large onion, finely chopped
4 garlic cloves, finely diced
1/2 cup chopped fresh fennel, approximately 2 bulbs
pinch of saffron
1/2 teaspoon black pepper plus more to taste
1 teaspoon chopped fresh thyme
1 jar LuLu Heirloom Tomato & Roasted Garlic Sauce
1/2 cup LuLu Roasted Tomato Harissa
1 quart fish or vegetable stock or broth, or water
1/2 pound Dungeness crab meat, picked over
2 tablespoons chopped fennel fronds (tops)
salt to taste
homemade crostini (see page 18)
1/2 cup LuLu Saffron & Garlic Rouille

Preparation:

Warm olive oil in a medium stockpot (approximately 3 quarts) over medium heat, and sauté onion, garlic and fennel until translucent, about 10 minutes. (Be sure that garlic doesn't turn brown or it will taste bitter.) Stir in saffron, pepper and thyme and cook, stirring for another 2 or 3 minutes.

Add LuLu Heirloom Tomato & Roasted Garlic Sauce, LuLu Roasted Tomato Harissa and stock (or water), and bring to a boil. Reduce heat and simmer soup for 45 minutes.

Gently stir crabmeat and fennel fronds into soup. Add salt and additional pepper to taste. (Alternatively, portion the crabmeat and fennel fronds into bowls and ladle the soup over them.)

To serve: ladle soup into individual bowls and garnish each bowl with a dollop of LuLu Saffron & Garlic Rouille. Serve with crostini and additional Rouille.

Note: Dungeness crabs are found throughout the waters off the West Coast from Alaska to Mexico. If you're in a region where fresh Dungeness are not available, substitute other fresh varieties such as Alaskan king crab, blue crab and stone crab, or even frozen crab.

Other LuLu Products: If LuLu Saffron & Garlic Rouille is not available, substitute LuLu Garlic Aioli.

Butternut Squash Soup with Lavender Honey

8 servings

Featuring: **LuLu Preserved Meyer Lemon, Fennel & Sage Marinade**
LuLu Essence of Lavender Honey

Ingredients:
1 butternut squash, about 2-1/2 pounds
4 tablespoons butter
1 onion, chopped
4 garlic cloves, minced
salt and pepper to taste
2 tablespoons extra virgin olive oil
2 tablespoons LuLu Preserved Meyer Lemon, Fennel & Sage Marinade
5 tablespoons LuLu Essence of Lavender Honey
2 bay leaves
6 sprigs plus 2 tablespoons chopped fresh thyme
8 cups chicken or vegetable stock or broth, or water
4 cups milk
1/2 cup crème fraîche
2 tablespoons chopped fresh parsley

Preparation:
Peel and seed squash and cut into 1-inch cubes .

Melt butter in a large stockpot (6 to 8 quarts) over medium-high heat. When butter begins to brown, stir in squash, onion, garlic, and salt and pepper, and cook for 10 minutes until onions are golden brown. Add olive oil, LuLu Preserved Meyer Lemon, Fennel & Sage Marinade, 2 tablespoons of LuLu Essence of Lavender Honey, bay leaves and thyme sprigs to stockpot and continue cooking for 4 more minutes, stirring occasionally.

Stir in stock and milk, and cover pot until liquid begins to simmer. Lower heat and cook uncovered for about 30 minutes until squash is tender. Remove from heat. Remove and discard thyme sprigs and bay leaves.

Using a hand blender, countertop blender or food processor, purée hot liquid and vegetables together until very smooth, puréeing in batches if necessary. Return soup to stockpot and keep warm. Taste and adjust salt and pepper.

continued

To serve: ladle soup into individual bowls and top each with 1 tablespoon crème fraîche. Drizzle about 1 teaspoon LuLu Essence of Lavender Honey over each bowl and garnish with pinches of chopped parsley and thyme.

Note: LuLu Marinades are more like "wet" spice rubs than other marinades which are thinned with water. Packed with flavorful ingredients blended together with olive and canola oils, LuLu Marinades are concentrated enough to be used as seasonings, as it is in this recipe.

Other LuLu Products: If LuLu Preserved Meyer Lemon, Fennel & Sage Marinade is not available, substitute LuLu Preserved Meyer Lemon & Rosemary Marinade.

Green Salad with Herbed Goat Cheese

4 to 6 servings

Featuring: **LuLu Herbes de Provence Seasoning**
LuLu Fig & Meyer Lemon Balsamic Vinegar

Ingredients: 8 ounces fresh goat cheese
1 tablespoon LuLu Herbes de Provence Seasoning
6 cups mixed salad greens
salt and pepper to taste
4 tablespoons LuLu Fig & Meyer Lemon Balsamic Vinegar
2 tablespoons extra virgin olive oil

Preparation: Take a spoonful of goat cheese and roll the cheese with your hands into a 1/2-inch ball. Repeat with remaining cheese, then roll each ball in LuLu Herbes de Provence Seasoning to lightly coat. Set aside. (Refrigerate if preparing the goat cheese balls in advance.)

Place salad greens into a large bowl and season with salt and pepper to taste. Toss greens with LuLu Fig & Meyer Lemon Balsamic Vinegar, then drizzle with olive oil and toss again.

Arrange the greens on a platter or individual plates and garnish with the goat cheese balls. Serve immediately.

Note: Goat cheese is also known as chèvre (literally meaning goat in French), and perhaps the most famous brand is Montrachet, which comes from the Burgundy region. For this recipe we recommend using any domestic or imported fresh (not aged), soft, mild-flavored goat's milk cheese.

Grilled Asparagus and Citrus Salad

4 to 6 servings

Featuring: **LuLu Citrus Grilling Sauce**
LuLu Fig & Tangerine Balsamic Vinegar

Ingredients:

1 pound asparagus, trimmed
3 tablespoons LuLu Citrus Grilling Sauce
2 cups hazelnuts
2 tangerines
7 cups (loosely-packed) mixed baby greens
2 tablespoons LuLu Fig & Tangerine Balsamic Vinegar
2 tablespoons extra virgin olive oil
salt and pepper to taste

Preparation:

Heat grill to medium-high. Preheat oven to 425°.

In a medium bowl, toss asparagus with LuLu Citrus Grilling Sauce and let asparagus marinate before grilling.

Arrange hazelnuts on a baking sheet in a single layer and toast in oven for 8 to 10 minutes. Remove from the oven and rub nuts in a clean dishtowel to remove skins. Allow hazelnuts to cool and then chop coarsely. Reserve 2 tablespoons chopped hazelnuts separately from the remaining hazelnuts.

Peel tangerines and cut around membranes into sections. (Cut tangerine sections are known as "supremes".) Set aside.

Grill asparagus on all sides a total of 4 to 5 minutes and remove from heat. Arrange asparagus spears like the spokes of a wheel on a large round plate.

In a large bowl, toss salad greens with half of the tangerine supremes, hazelnuts, LuLu Fig & Tangerine Balsamic Vinegar, olive oil, and salt and pepper. Pile salad in the middle of platter over asparagus. Garnish platter with remaining tangerine supremes and reserved hazelnuts.

Note: This is a recipe for early spring when fresh asparagus first appears in the market and fresh tangerines are still available. If tangerines are not available, substitute navel oranges.

Other LuLu Products: If LuLu Fig & Tangerine Balsamic Vinegar is not available, substitute another LuLu Balsamic Vinegar.

Frittata with Marinated Leeks

2 servings

Featuring: **LuLu Basil Pistou**
LuLu Marinated Leeks
LuLu Preserved Meyer Lemon & Artichoke Vinaigrette
LuLu Green Olive Tapenade

Ingredients: 2 tablespoons butter
4 eggs
1 tablespoon LuLu Basil Pistou
1 tablespoon LuLu Marinated Leeks
6 cherry tomatoes, cut in half
1/3 cup diced fontina cheese
salt and freshly-ground black pepper to taste
approximately 4 to 5 cups mixed salad greens
3 tablespoons LuLu Preserved Meyer Lemon & Artichoke Vinaigrette
2 tablespoons LuLu Green Olive Tapenade for garnish

Preparation: Preheat oven to 350°.

Place a large skillet over medium heat and add butter. In a small bowl, lightly beat eggs with LuLu Basil Pistou and pour into skillet when the butter has melted. Quickly stir the eggs while still loose, fold in LuLu Marinated Leeks, tomato halves, and fontina cheese, and season with salt and pepper. Allow frittata to set undisturbed; do not stir it anymore.

Place the skillet in the oven and bake until fully cooked, approximately 8 minutes.

While frittata is baking, toss salad greens with LuLu Preserved Meyer Lemon & Artichoke Vinaigrette.

When frittata has finished baking, divide it in half and slide each half onto a plate. Spoon half of LuLu Green Olive Tapenade onto each frittata half and serve with salad.

| Note: | A frittata is an Italian version of an omelet. The difference is that additional ingredients are stirred and cooked into the eggs as opposed to the eggs being folded around the other ingredients. Also frittatas are finished cooking by baking in an oven. |

| Other LuLu Products: | If LuLu Basil Pistou is not available, or for a zestier flavor, substitute LuLu Romesco Sauce or LuLu Roasted Tomato Harissa. If LuLu Marinated Leeks are not available, substitute LuLu Truffled Artichoke Tapenade. Lastly, if LuLu Green Olive Tapenade is not available, substitute LuLu Olive Tapenade or LuLu Sun-Dried Tomato & Porcini Tapenade. |

Grilled Shrimp with Romesco

4 to 6 servings

Featuring: **LuLu Romesco Sauce**
               LuLu Herbes de Provence Seasoning
               LuLu Spicy Corn Remoulade

Ingredients: 1 pound large shrimp (26 -30 count), deveined with peel left on
               2 tablespoons LuLu Romesco Sauce
               1/2 teaspoon LuLu Herbes de Provence Seasoning
               1/2 tablespoon extra virgin olive oil
               1 jar LuLu Spicy Corn Remoulade
               1/2 head butter lettuce, individual leaves rinsed and patted dry
               1 tablespoon minced chives

Preparation: Heat grill.

               In a medium bowl, toss shrimp with 1 tablespoon LuLu Romesco Sauce,
               LuLu Herbes de Provence Seasoning and olive oil until the shrimp are
               evenly coated.

               Grill shrimp for 2 minutes on each side. Remove from grill and toss shrimp
               with remaining Romesco and set aside.

               To serve: line a plate or bowl with butter lettuce leaves. Place LuLu Spicy
               Corn Remoulade into a small bowl in the center of the plate. Surround
               bowl of Remoulade with grilled shrimp and sprinkle with chives. Serve
               immediately.

Note: *Remoulade is a French sauce made with mayonnaise, capers, anchovies and gherkins. LuLu Spicy Corn Remoulade is our spin on this traditional condiment, using fresh cream and uniquely American ingredients including corn and red chilies.*

Sweet and Spicy Chicken Skewers

4 to 6 servings

Featuring: **LuLu Mustard with Harissa**
               LuLu Sweet & Spicy Tomato Grilling Glaze

Ingredients: wooden skewers (soak in water for 1 hour beforehand to prevent them
                  from burning during grilling)
               2 boneless, skinless chicken breasts
               4 tablespoons LuLu Mustard with Harissa
               1 tablespoon extra virgin olive oil
               salt and pepper to taste
               1/2 cup LuLu Sweet & Spicy Tomato Grilling Glaze

Preparation: Heat grill or broiler.

               Rinse chicken breasts and pat dry. Cut chicken into 1/2-inch pieces. In a
               small bowl combine LuLu Mustard with Harissa, olive oil, salt and pepper,
               and then toss chicken with the mustard mixture.

               Thread 2-3 pieces of chicken onto each skewer. Grill or broil skewers for
               about 2 minutes on each side until cooked through.

               Serve chicken skewers with LuLu Sweet & Spicy Tomato Grilling Glaze on
               the side as a dipping sauce.

Note:	To adjust recipe to 2 entrée portions, cut chicken into 1-inch pieces and cook an additional 1 to 2 minutes on each side. Serve over rice or couscous.
Other LuLu Products:	This versatile recipe can be prepared using any one of LuLu's Grilling Sauces and Glazes and any one of LuLu's Mustards.

Scallop and Pancetta Skewers

6 servings

Featuring: **LuLu Fig Balsamic Grilling Sauce**
                  LuLu Fennel. Olive & Onion Confit

Ingredients: wooden skewers (soak in water for 1 hour beforehand to prevent them from burning during grilling)
3 pounds sea scallops
1 - 6 ounce piece of pancetta (Italian bacon)
salt and pepper to taste
1/2 bottle LuLu Fig Balsamic Grilling Sauce
1 tablespoon extra virgin olive oil
1/2 jar LuLu Fennel, Olive & Onion Confit

Preparation: Rinse scallops and pat dry. Cut pancetta into 3/4-inch cubes.

Thread one pancetta cube onto a skewer followed by a scallop. Thread two more scallops and pancetta cubes onto the same skewer, alternating, so you end up with three of each on a skewer. Repeat with additional skewers until all the remaining scallops and pancetta are used.

Arrange skewers in a baking pan large enough to hold them flat in one layer. Season with salt and pepper and pour LuLu Fig Balsamic Grilling Sauce over them. Gently turn the skewers so they are evenly coated with the sauce. Drizzle with olive oil, cover skewers and refrigerate for 45 minutes.

Heat grill to high heat and grill skewers for 2 minutes on each side.

Serve skewers accompanied by LuLu Fennel, Olive & Onion Confit.

Note: There are two types of scallops sold in markets, sea and bay scallops.
Sea scallops are larger and more readily available, and better withstand
high heat cooking methods like grilling. Bay scallops are very small and
delicate, and are usually prepared in a quick sauté.

Other LuLu   If LuLu Fig Balsamic Grilling Sauce is not available, substitute LuLu
Products: Lavender Honey Grilling Sauce.

Lamb Brochettes
with Red Onion Salad and Olive Tapenade

4 servings

Featuring: **LuLu Citrus Grilling Sauce**
LuLu Olive Tapenade

Ingredients: wooden skewers (soak in water for 1 hour beforehand to prevent them
from burning during grilling)
1 large red onion
3 tablespoons freshly-squeezed lemon juice
2 tablespoons extra virgin olive oil
4 tablespoons chopped fresh parsley
1 pound lamb sirloin or lamb shoulder
salt and pepper to taste
1/2 cup LuLu Citrus Grilling Sauce
1 tablespoon chopped fresh thyme
1/4 cup LuLu Olive Tapenade

Preparation: Heat grill on high heat.

Prepare onion salad: slice onion as thinly as possible and toss in a bowl
with lemon juice, olive oil, 2 tablespoons parsley, and salt and pepper to
taste. Set aside.

Cut lamb into thin strips about 3/4 inches wide by 3 inches long. Thread
each strip onto a wooden skewer and place on a baking sheet or similar
tray in a single layer. Season with salt and pepper and brush both sides
with LuLu Citrus Grilling Sauce. Grill for about 2 minutes per side.

To serve: place onion salad on a large plate or serving platter and
arrange hot lamb skewers in one layer on top of salad. Sprinkle lamb
with remaining parsley and thyme, and then spoon LuLu Olive Tapenade
over lamb. Serve immediately.

Note: Preparing the lamb by cutting it into thin strips will ensure that the cooked meat will be tender.

Other LuLu Products: If LuLu Citrus Grilling Sauce is not available, substitute LuLu Pomegranate Grilling Glaze.

Salmon Burgers with Mediterranean Salad

6 servings

Featuring: **LuLu Green Olive Tapenade**
              LuLu Saffron & Garlic Rouille

Ingredients: 1 lemon
                2 pounds skinless salmon fillets, bones removed
                1 cup plus 3 tablespoons chopped fresh parsley
                1 tablespoon minced fresh tarragon
                1 tablespoon minced fresh chives
                2 tablespoons diced shallots
                2 tablespoons LuLu Green Olive Tapenade
                1/2 teaspoon each salt and pepper plus more to taste
                6 cups mixed salad greens
                1 15-1/2 oz. can garbanzo beans, drained
                2 cups thinly sliced red onion
                2 tablespoons extra virgin olive oil
                6 hamburger buns or soft round rolls
                6 tablespoons LuLu Saffron & Garlic Rouille
                1 bunch fresh watercress, rinsed, patted dry and tough stems removed

Preparation: Heat grill to high heat.

                Remove zest from lemon with a vegetable peeler in long strips, dice the
                zest finely and set aside. Squeeze juice from lemon through a strainer
                into a small bowl and set aside.

                Chop salmon into a small dice and place into a large bowl. Add to
                salmon reserved lemon zest, 1 tablespoon parsley, tarragon, chives,
                shallots, LuLu Green Olive Tapenade, and salt and pepper, and gently
                blend together. Form salmon mixture into 6 patties.

                Place salmon patties onto grill and cook for about 3 minutes on each
                side.

                Toss salad greens with garbanzo beans, red onion, and 1 cup parsley.
                Dress salad with reserved lemon juice, olive oil, and salt and pepper and
                set aside.

continued

Spread LuLu Saffron & Garlic Rouille on both sides of each hamburger bun. Divide watercress into 6 portions and place onto the bottom halves of each of 6 buns. Place salmon burgers on top of watercress, sprinkle with remaining parsley, and cover with top bun.

To serve: place each salmon burger on a plate and arrange the salad alongside the burger.

Other LuLu Products: *If LuLu Green Olive Tapenade is not available, substitute another LuLu Tapenade. If LuLu Saffron & Garlic Rouille is not available, substitute another LuLu Mayonnaise.*

Grilled Sausage Sandwiches with Caramelized Onions

6 servings

Featuring: **LuLu Fig Balsamic Vinegar**
LuLu Mustard with Herbes de Provence

Ingredients:
1/2 cup extra virgin olive oil
1 red onion, thinly sliced
1 yellow onion, thinly sliced
3 tablespoons LuLu Fig Balsamic Vinegar
6 uncooked sausages, your choice of pork, beef, chicken or turkey
6 baked individual pizza crusts (such as Boboli)
salt and pepper to taste
2 tablespoons LuLu Mustard with Herbes de Provence
12 sprigs fresh rosemary

Preparation:
To caramelize onions: in a large sauté pan heat 1/4 cup olive oil over medium heat. Add both red and yellow onions and sauté for 10 minutes until onions begin to brown, then reduce heat to low and continue cooking for an additional 35 minutes, stirring occasionally. Remove pan from heat and stir in LuLu Fig Balsamic Vinegar. Set aside.

Heat grill to medium heat.

Pierce sausages with a fork (to let steam escape while cooking) and grill for 8 minutes until browned and cooked through. Remove from grill and set aside.

Brush remaining olive oil onto both sides of pizza crusts. Sprinkle with salt and pepper and grill for 2 to 3 minutes on each side until browned.

With pizza crusts still warm, spread LuLu Mustard with Herbes de Provence over half of one side of each crust. Divide caramelized onions into six portions, and spread each portion onto a pizza crust, leaving a 2-inch edge all around. Place a cooked sausage onto each crust and fold the crust around it. Skewer each sandwich with 2 sprigs of rosemary and serve warm.

Note: You can substitute homemade pizza dough for the baked pizza crusts.
Form dough into 6 small rounds and brush each on both sides with olive
oil (you may need additional oil). After sausages have finished cooking,
grill dough about 4 minutes on each side until golden.

Heirloom Tomato BLT

6 servings

Featuring:	**LuLu French Mayonnaise with Dijon Mustard**

Ingredients:

24 to 30 slices bacon
2 loaves levain or other sourdough bread rounds
2 pounds heirloom tomatoes
1/2 head butter lettuce
salt and pepper to taste
8 tablespoons LuLu French Mayonnaise with Dijon Mustard
12 fresh basil leaves
long toothpicks for assembling sandwiches

Preparation:

Prepare bacon: cook in a sauté pan over medium heat until brown and crispy. (Alternatively, prepare bacon in a broiler or a microwave.) Place bacon slices on paper towels to drain excess fat and set aside.

While bacon is cooking, cut bread into 18 1/2-inch thick slices. Toast bread and set aside.

Cut heirloom tomatoes into thin slices and sprinkle with salt and pepper. Separate leaves of lettuce and rinse and spin dry.

To assemble sandwiches: spread one side of each slice of toast with LuLu French Mayonnaise with Dijon Mustard. Divide tomato slices into 12 portions. Arrange one portion of tomato slices on top of mayonnaise on 1 bread slice. Top tomatoes with 4 basil leaves and cover with another slice of toast with the mayonnaise side facing down. Spread additional LuLu French Mayonnaise with Dijon Mustard onto the top of this slice of toast and layer with a few lettuce leaves, another portion of tomato slices and 4 or 5 strips of bacon. Cover with a third slice of toast with the mayonnaise side facing down. Secure sandwich with 2 long toothpicks.

Repeat with remaining ingredients to assemble 5 more sandwiches. Cut each sandwich in half between the toothpicks and serve.

Note: Heirloom tomatoes are growing in popularity throughout the U.S. Once found only at farmers' markets, you can now find heirlooms during the summer in many grocery stores. Look for an assortment of colors and shapes with fanciful names such as Brandywine, Green Zebra, and Banana Fingers.

Pasta

Pappardelle Pasta
with Morel Mushrooms and Marinated Leeks

4 to 6 servings

Featuring: **LuLu Marinated Leeks**

Ingredients: 1 tablespoon butter
                  1 tablespoon extra virgin olive oil
                  2 teaspoons chopped garlic
                  1-1/2 cups fresh morel mushrooms, washed thoroughly (or your favorite
                     specialty mushrooms, cut into pieces if large)
                  8 ounces fresh spinach leaves
                  1/2 jar LuLu Marinated Leeks
                  salt and pepper to taste
                  1 pound fresh pappardelle pasta
                  1/4 pound aged Asiago cheese, either shaved or grated

Preparation: In a large sauté pan, warm butter over medium-high heat until brown.
                  Add olive oil and then stir in garlic and morels. Stir occasionally until
                  mushrooms are tender (about 5 minutes). Stir in spinach and LuLu
                  Marinated Leeks and season to taste with salt and pepper.

                  Meanwhile, cook pappardelle according to package directions in
                  salted boiling water until al dente. Drain pasta, reserving 1/4 cup pasta
                  water, and immediately toss pasta in a large bowl with the warm
                  mushroom mixture and reserved pasta water.

                  Serve from large bowl or platter, or divide onto individual plates and top
                  with Asiago cheese. Serve immediately.

Note: *Although you can substitute dried for fresh pasta, there are differences between them. Fresh pasta, often made with eggs, is more delicate and usually paired with lighter sauces. Dried pasta, especially imported brands, frequently contains semolina which gives it a chewy texture. Since dried pasta expands during cooking, use half the amount when substituting for fresh pasta.*

Other LuLu
Products: *If LuLu Marinated Leeks are not available, substitute a LuLu Tapenade.*

Orecchiette with Mustard Grilled Chicken and Broccoli Rabe

4 to 6 servings

Featuring: **LuLu Mustard & Herbes de Provence Grilling Sauce**
LuLu Sun-Dried Tomato & Porcini Tapenade

Ingredients:

4 boneless, skinless chicken breasts
1/2 cup LuLu Mustard & Herbes de Provence Grilling Sauce
1/2 pound dried orecchiette pasta
3 tablespoons extra virgin olive oil
2 garlic cloves, sliced into thin slivers
1 bunch broccoli rabe, rinsed and trimmed
1/4 cup LuLu Sun-Dried Tomato & Porcini Tapenade
1 cup chicken stock or broth
salt and pepper to taste
freshly grated Parmesan cheese for garnish if desired

Preparation:

Heat grill to medium-high heat.

Rinse chicken breasts and pat dry. Brush LuLu Mustard & Herbes de Provence Grilling Sauce all over chicken. Grill chicken for about 4 minutes on each side until cooked through. Remove from heat and set aside.

Meanwhile, cook orecchiette according to package directions in salted boiling water until al dente.

While pasta is cooking heat extra virgin olive oil in a large sauté pan over medium-high heat. Stir in garlic and sauté for approximately 2 minutes, stirring constantly, until garlic is golden. Add broccoli rabe and sauté for approximately 5 more minutes until tender, stirring occasionally. Increase heat to high, stir in LuLu Sun-Dried Tomato & Porcini Tapenade and chicken stock and cook an additional 2 minutes.

Drain the pasta and stir it into the tapenade mixture, cooking an additional 2 to 3 minutes. Taste and adjust salt and pepper. Cut chicken breasts on the diagonal into 1/2-inch slices.

continued

To serve: spoon pasta into individual serving bowls, or onto a large platter. Arrange chicken breasts on top of pasta and top with Parmesan cheese if desired. Serve immediately.

Note:

Orecchiette, literally translated from Italian as "little ears", is a small disk-shaped pasta. This recipe also works well with other "short" pasta shapes, such as penne (hollow cylinder with pointed ends) and conchigliette (small sea shell-shaped pasta).

Angel Hair Pasta with Seafood and Ratatouille

4 to 6 servings

Featuring: **LuLu Classic Ratatouille Provençal**

Ingredients:
1/4 cup extra virgin olive oil
1 pound clams, scrubbed
1-1/2 jars LuLu Classic Ratatouille Provençal
3/4 pound swordfish or halibut fillets, skin removed and cut into
  1-inch cubes
salt and pepper to taste
3/4 pound prawns, peeled and deveined
4 tablespoons chopped fresh parsley
1 pound fresh angel hair pasta

Preparation:
Heat olive oil in a large sauté pan over medium heat. Add clams and cook for 2 to 3 minutes, occasionally shaking pan to stir the clams. Add LuLu Classic Ratatouille Provençal and 1/2 jar water and stir to combine.

Stir in swordfish or halibut cubes, season with salt and pepper and sauté for 3 minutes. Stir in prawns and sauté for 5 more minutes. Stir in 2 tablespoons parsley, cover and remove from heat.

Cook angel hair pasta according to package directions in salted boiling water until al dente, drain and then stir into sauté pan with the seafood mixture. Cook an additional 1 to 2 minutes until heated through.

Spoon pasta with seafood onto a large serving platter or into individual bowls. Sprinkle with remaining chopped parsley and serve immediately.

Note: You can substitute other shellfish for the clams and prawns, such as mussels or scallops, and other white, firm fish for the swordfish or halibut, such as scrod or cod.

Other LuLu Products: If LuLu Classic Ratatouille Provençal is not available, substitute LuLu Provençal Grilled Vegetable Sauce.

Linguine
with Basil Pistou, Green Beans and Potatoes
6 to 8 servings

Featuring: **LuLu Basil Pistou**

Ingredients: 5 garlic cloves
                  2 pounds small red potatoes
                  10 sprigs fresh thyme
                  salt and pepper to taste
                  2 pounds fresh linguine pasta
                  1/2 pound green string beans
                  3 tablespoons extra virgin olive oil
                  1 jar LuLu Basil Pistou
                  1/2 cup freshly grated Parmesan cheese

Preparation: Smash 2 of the garlic cloves and place them into a large pot with the
                  potatoes, thyme sprigs, salt and pepper and add cold water to cover.
                  Bring to a boil, reduce heat and simmer until tender but not mushy,
                  about 15 minutes. Drain potatoes and set aside to cool.

                  Cook linguine according to package directions in salted boiling water
                  until al dente. Reserve 1 cup of the pasta cooking water, and then drain
                  linguine. Set aside.

                  Meanwhile, bring a small pot of water to a boil. Trim ends from the string
                  beans and blanch them in boiling water for 3 to 4 minutes. Drain and
                  submerge beans into an ice water bath. When beans have cooled,
                  drain and set aside.

                  Cut cooled potatoes in half or into 1/4-inch thick slices.

                  Slice remaining 3 garlic cloves into thin slivers. In a large sauté pan over
                  medium-high heat, sauté slivered garlic in olive oil until golden, about
                  1 minute. Stir in the pasta, string beans, and potatoes, and season with
                  salt and pepper. Stir in LuLu Basil Pistou plus reserved pasta cooking
                  water and simmer for 2 to 3 minutes until heated through.

                  Serve pasta warm topped with freshly grated Parmesan cheese.

Note: Although most Americans would not think of combining pasta and potatoes, this recipe is a version of a traditional French recipe prepared with haricots vert, literally translated as "beans green". Use the smallest, most tender green beans that you can find.

If small red potatoes are not available, substitute large red potatoes cut into halves or quarters. If fresh linguine is not available, substitute 1 pound dried linguine.

Other LuLu Products: If LuLu Basil Pistou is not available, substitute a LuLu Tapenade.

Pastina with Summer Squash and Goat Cheese

4 to 6 servings

Featuring: **LuLu Spicy Corn Remoulade**
               LuLu Basil Pistou

Ingredients: 1 pound summer squash, such as pattypan, crookneck, or zucchini
               1 pound pastina
               salt
               2 tablespoons extra virgin olive oil
               3 garlic cloves, sliced into thin slivers
               1 jar LuLu Spicy Corn Remoulade
               2 tablespoons crème fraîche
               3 tablespoons LuLu Basil Pistou
               3 ounces goat cheese, broken into large pieces
               3 tablespoons chopped fresh parsley

Preparation: Prepare squash: cut off ends from squash, cut in half lengthwise and
               then slice across into 1/2-inch thick half moons. Set aside.

               Cook pastina according to package directions in salted boiling water
               until al dente. Reserve 1 cup of the pasta cooking water, and then drain
               pastina through a fine mesh sieve. Set aside.

               Heat an ovenproof serving platter in a warm oven.

               Meanwhile, heat olive oil in a large sauté pan over medium-high heat.
               Stir in garlic and squash and sauté 3 to 4 minutes, until just turning
               golden. Remove from heat and stir pastina into the squash. Stir in LuLu
               Spicy Corn Remoulade, reserved pasta cooking water, crème fraiche,
               and LuLu Basil Pistou.

               Spoon pastina and squash mixture onto the heated serving platter and
               garnish with goat cheese and chopped parsley. Serve immediately.

Note: *Pastina means "tiny dough" in Italian and refers to any small-sized pasta shape such as orzo or acini de pepe. These small shapes are generally used in soups.*

Other LuLu
Products: *If LuLu Basil Pistou is not available, substitute a LuLu Tapenade.*

Ravioli with Truffled Artichoke Tapenade

4 to 6 servings

Featuring: **LuLu Truffled Artichoke Tapenade**

Ingredients:
2 pounds fresh or frozen ravioli or tortellini (any flavor)
salt
3/4 cup chicken stock or broth
2/3 cup chopped fresh parsley
freshly ground black pepper
4 tablespoons LuLu Truffled Artichoke Tapenade
1/2 cup thinly-shaved Parmesan cheese

Preparation:
Cook ravioli according to package directions in salted boiling water until al dente.

Meanwhile, heat chicken stock in a large saucepan over medium heat. When the ravioli are done, drain and add to the chicken stock.

Place 2 tablespoons chopped parsley into each of four individual pasta bowls. Divide ravioli into the four bowls and pour stock over the ravioli. Sprinkle with freshly ground black pepper. Top each dish with 1 tablespoon LuLu Truffled Artichoke Tapenade.

Garnish each serving with remaining chopped parsley and shaved Parmesan and serve immediately.

Note: In any recipe requiring stock or broth, it is always best to use homemade, which can be kept in your freezer until you need it. Alternatively, look for frozen broth or concentrate, or canned broth with as little salt or MSG (monosodium glutamate) as possible.

"Free-Form" Lamb Bolognese Lasagne

4 to 6 servings

Featuring: **LuLu Provençal Roasted Tomato Sauce**
LuLu Basil Pistou

Ingredients:

4 tablespoons extra virgin olive oil
2 pounds ground lamb
salt and pepper to taste
6 garlic cloves, sliced into thin slivers
2 onions, diced
1 cup LuLu Provençal Roasted Tomato Sauce
1/2 cup tomato paste
1-1/2 cups red wine
1-1/2 cups beef stock or broth
12 dried lasagne noodles (about 1/2 pound)
1/2 cup cream or milk
1 tablespoon chopped fresh oregano
1 tablespoon chopped fresh rosemary
1 tablespoon chopped fresh sage
3 tablespoons chopped fresh parsley
1-1/2 cups ricotta cheese
1/2 cup shaved Pecorino Romano cheese
6 tablespoons LuLu Basil Pistou

Preparation:

Prepare lamb Bolognese: heat 3 tablespoons olive oil in a large sauté pan over medium-high heat. Add ground lamb, season with salt and pepper, and cook for 10 minutes, breaking apart the meat with the back of a spoon as it browns. Remove the lamb with a slotted spoon and set aside. Pour off all but 2 tablespoons fat from the pan.

Add garlic and onion to pan and sauté for 5 minutes, stirring, until translucent. Stir in LuLu Provençal Roasted Tomato Sauce, tomato paste, red wine and beef stock and then stir in cooked lamb. Reduce heat to low and simmer for 45 minutes.

Meanwhile, cook lasagne noodles according to package directions in salted boiling water until al dente. Drain pasta, cut each noodle in half crosswise, and set aside.

continued

After the lamb sauce has finished simmering, stir in cream, oregano, rosemary, sage and 1 tablespoon parsley. Remove pan from heat.

To assemble: warm six ovenproof plates in a 200° oven. Spoon 2 tablespoons ricotta onto a warm plate and top with a noodle, pressing it down into the ricotta. Spread 2 more tablespoons ricotta onto noodle and top with 4 tablespoons lamb Bolognese. Repeat with two more layers and finish with a noodle on top. Place in oven while assembling remaining portions.

To serve: remove lasagnes from oven and sprinkle with remaining parsley and Pecorino cheese. Top each with 1 tablespoon LuLu Basil Pistou, and then drizzle with remaining olive oil. Serve immediately.

Butternut Squash Risotto

4 to 6 servings

Featuring:	**LuLu Preserved Meyer Lemon & Rosemary Marinade** **LuLu Cherry Balsamic Vinegar**

Ingredients:
- 1 butternut squash
- 6 cups vegetable or chicken stock or broth
- 1 cup extra virgin olive oil
- 1 cup diced shallots (or white or yellow onion)
- 1/2 jar LuLu Preserved Meyer Lemon & Rosemary Marinade
- 1 pound (2 cups) Arborio or Carnaroli rice
- 1 cup white wine
- 1/2 cup crème fraîche
- 2 tablespoons LuLu Cherry Balsamic Vinegar
- 2 tablespoons chopped fresh parsley
- 6 tablespoons freshly grated Parmesan cheese

Preparation:

Peel and seed squash and cut into a 1/2-inch dice.

Heat stock in a medium pot. In a separate large pot with a heavy bottom, heat olive oil over medium-high heat. Stir in shallots and sauté for 3 to 5 minutes until golden, then stir in LuLu Preserved Meyer Lemon & Rosemary Marinade. Add the rice and cook, stirring, 3 minutes. Stir in wine, and when it is mostly absorbed stir in 1 cup hot stock.

Continue stirring while cooking, until almost all the stock is absorbed. Repeat with 1 more cup stock. Stir in chopped squash, add one more cup stock and stir until it is absorbed. Repeat this process until the risotto is al dente (rice will be firm to the tooth and slightly creamy). Remove pot from heat and stir in the crème fraîche.

To serve: spoon risotto into a large serving bowl or into individual bowls. Drizzle with LuLu Cherry Balsamic Vinegar and sprinkle with parsley and Parmesan cheese. Serve immediately.

Note: *Risotto, originally an Italian recipe, is usually prepared with Arborio rice, though other types of rice are suitable for this dish. Risotto rice has short, fat grains that break apart during the cooking process, resulting in its signature creamy texture.*

Sunchoke Risotto with Crimini Mushrooms

4 to 6 servings

Featuring: **LuLu Preserved Meyer Lemon in Olive Oil**

Ingredients:
8 cups vegetable or chicken stock or broth
1/2 cup plus 2 tablespoons extra virgin olive oil
1 cup diced shallots (or white or yellow onion)
1 pound (2 cups) Arborio or Carnaroli rice
1 cup white wine
1-1/2 pounds sunchokes (Jerusalem artichokes), peeled and chopped
3/4 pound crimini mushrooms (or your favorite specialty mushroom),
  thinly sliced
2 cups cooked, shredded pork (or chicken)
1-1/2 cups frozen peas, thawed
Optional: 1/2 cup pea shoots (optional)
1 tablespoon LuLu Preserved Meyer Lemon in Olive Oil
1/2 cup chopped fresh thyme
1/2 cup chopped fresh parsley
3/4 cup freshly grated Parmesan cheese
salt and freshly ground black pepper to taste

Preparation:
Heat stock. In a separate large pot with a heavy bottom, heat 1/2 cup olive oil over medium-high heat. Stir in shallots and sauté for 3 to 5 minutes until golden. Stir in rice and cook, stirring, 3 minutes. Stir in wine, and when it is mostly absorbed stir in 1 cup hot stock.

Continue stirring while cooking, until almost all the stock is absorbed. Repeat with 1 more cup stock. Stir in sunchokes, add one more cup stock and stir until it is absorbed. Repeat this process until the risotto is al dente (rice will be firm to the tooth and slightly creamy); you should have about 2 cups of stock remaining.

While risotto is cooking heat remaining olive oil in a sauté pan over medium heat and sauté mushrooms until soft, approximately 10 minutes. Stir in shredded pork and 1-1/2 cups stock and simmer for 5 minutes. Stir in peas and cook an additional minute. If using pea shoots, stir them in with the peas.

continued

When the risotto is al dente, stir in LuLu Preserved Meyer Lemon in Olive Oil, thyme and parsley, and then stir in Parmesan cheese. Taste and season with salt and pepper.

To serve: spoon risotto into 6 warmed individual bowls. With the back of a spoon make a well in the center of the risotto and spoon the mushroom mixture into the well. Drizzle the remaining stock over risotto around the edges of the bowls and serve immediately.

Note: *Sunchokes are also known as Jerusalem artichokes, despite the fact that they are not related to artichokes and do not come from Jerusalem. Sunchokes are a tuber and are related to sunflowers. Be sure not to chop them too far in advance, or they will discolor.*

Wood Grills
& Sautés

Tuna Au Poivre
with Shellfish and Stemperata Sauce

8 servings

Featuring: **LuLu Au Poivre Marinade**
LuLu Sweet Pepper Stemperata Sauce

Ingredients:
non-stick vegetable oil spray
8 tuna fillets about 1-inch thick (approximately 2 pounds)
1 tablespoon sea salt
4 tablespoons LuLu Au Poivre Marinade
2 cups LuLu Sweet Pepper Stemperata Sauce
1 cup fish stock or clam juice
1/2 pound assorted shellfish, such as clams, mussels, prawns, and/or
   scallops, cleaned and/or scrubbed as needed
2 tablespoons chopped fresh parsley
Suggested accompaniments: pasta (we like orecchiette) or roasted
   potatoes

Preparation:
Prepare grill by lightly coating grates with non-stick vegetable oil spray.
Heat grill.

Rinse and pat dry the tuna fillets. Season tuna all over first with salt and
then with LuLu Au Poivre Marinade; be sure to lightly press marinade into
surface of fillets.

Grill tuna for 5 minutes on one side. Carefully turn fillets over and
continue cooking for about 5 more minutes, until tuna is cooked through.
Remove from grill and place onto a large platter.

While tuna is grilling, heat LuLu Sweet Pepper Stemperata Sauce with fish
stock in a large sauté pan. Add shellfish to pan, cover and reduce heat
to a simmer, and cook shellfish for about 4 minutes; clam and mussel
shells will have opened (discard shells that are not opened) and prawns
and scallops will be opaque and firm.

continued

To serve: pour sauce over tuna fillets and arrange shellfish all around. Sprinkle platter with chopped parsley and serve immediately with pasta or roasted potatoes.

Note: Alternatively, the tuna can be prepared by searing in a large sauté pan with a little bit of extra virgin olive oil.

Mustard Grilled Rib-Eye Steaks with Oven-Fried Potatoes

6 servings

Featuring: **LuLu Mustard with Harissa**
LuLu Goat Cheese & Olive Vinaigrette

Ingredients:
1-1/2 pounds Yukon gold potatoes
3 tablespoons plus 2 teaspoons extra virgin olive oil
salt and pepper to taste
2 tablespoons chopped fresh parsley
2 tablespoons chopped fresh thyme
3 double-thick (about 3 inches) rib-eye steaks
4 tablespoons LuLu Mustard with Harissa
1 bunch watercress
2 cups cherry tomatoes, halved
1 tablespoon LuLu Goat Cheese & Olive Vinaigrette

Preparation:
Preheat oven to 375°.

Cut potatoes into wedges, toss with 3 tablespoons olive oil and sprinkle with salt and pepper. Place in a single layer on a baking sheet and bake 25 minutes until golden. When potatoes are done, remove from oven and toss in a bowl with parsley and thyme. Set aside and keep warm.

Meanwhile, heat grill to medium heat. Spread LuLu Mustard with Harissa all over steaks and sprinkle with salt and pepper. Grill steaks over medium heat for 4 minutes, then rotate each steak 90° and continue grilling on the same side for 4 more minutes. Flip steaks to cook on the opposite side for 4 minutes, and again rotate steaks 90° and grill for 4 more minutes; steaks will be medium-rare. (Rotating the steaks will result in cross-hatched grill marks.) Let steaks rest for 10 minutes before slicing.

Rinse and spin dry the watercress and remove any tough stems. In a bowl toss watercress with cherry tomatoes, LuLu Goat Cheese & Olive Vinaigrette and remaining olive oil.

continued

To serve: slice steaks across the grain into 1/4-inch thick slices and divide onto six individual plates. Place potatoes onto plates and arrange salad next to potatoes. Serve immediately.

Note:	*Rib-eye steaks are the boneless, very tender cut from the cow's rib section, between the chuck and the short loin. If you prefer your steak more well-done, grill for an additional minute or two on each side. Remember that the steaks will continue cooking while resting before slicing.*
Other LuLu Products:	*If LuLu Mustard with Harissa is not available, substitute another LuLu Mustard.*

Citrus Grilled Salmon
with Cucumber, Grape and Almond Salad

4 to 6 servings

Featuring: **LuLu Citrus Grilling Sauce**
             LuLu Truffle Honey & Meyer Lemon Vinaigrette

Ingredients: 6 salmon fillets, about 6 ounces each
               1/3 cup LuLu Citrus Grilling Sauce
               3 English cucumbers
               4 cups green seedless grapes, cut in half
               2 cups thinly sliced radishes
               1 cup thinly sliced red onion
               3 tablespoons LuLu Truffle Honey & Meyer Lemon Vinaigrette
               salt and pepper to taste
               1 cup sliced almonds, lightly toasted
               chopped fresh parsley for garnish

Preparation: Four to six hours before serving time, rinse salmon fillets under cold,
               running water, and pat dry. Place fillets into a sealable plastic bag and
               pour LuLu Citrus Grilling Sauce over them. Allow salmon to marinate for
               4 to 6 hours.

               About 30 minutes before serving time, heat grill. (Alternatively, you can
               prepare salmon under a broiler.)

               While grill is heating, prepare salad. Cut ends from cucumbers and cut
               in half horizontally (you will have 6 long halves from the 3 cucumbers).
               Remove seeds with a spoon and slice thinly, leaving peel on.

               In a large bowl, gently toss sliced cucumbers with grapes, radishes and
               red onion. Dress salad with LuLu Truffle Honey & Meyer Lemon Vinaigrette
               and toss gently again. Taste salad and season with salt and pepper if
               desired. Set salad aside.

               Season salmon fillets on both sides with salt and pepper, and grill over
               medium-high heat for about 4 minutes on each side. Remove from grill.

               continued

To serve: place one salmon fillet on each plate and spoon salad alongside. Garnish salad with toasted almonds and sprinkle salmon with chopped parsley. Serve immediately.

Note:

There continues to be controversy between wild vs. farmed salmon. One argument is that wild salmon is overfished and that salmon could become extinct. Others counter that farmed salmon contain high levels of toxins, and aquaculture methods are destructive to the environment. Flavorwise, we prefer fresh wild salmon and urge consumers to patronize fishmongers that know the source of their supplies.

Lavender Honey Grilled Chicken with Basil Potato Galettes

4 servings

Featuring:
LuLu Basil Pistou
LuLu Lavender Honey Grilling Sauce
LuLu Truffle Honey & Meyer Lemon Vinaigrette

Ingredients:
4 boneless, skinless chicken breasts
1/2 bottle LuLu Lavender Honey Grilling Sauce
4 Yukon gold potatoes
2 tablespoons LuLu Basil Pistou
salt and pepper to taste
1/3 cup canola or vegetable oil
5 cups mixed salad greens
3 tablespoons LuLu Truffle Honey & Meyer Lemon Vinaigrette

Preparation:
Marinate chicken: place chicken breasts into a sealable plastic bag and pour LuLu Lavender Honey Grilling Sauce over them. Close bag and place in refrigerator while preparing galettes.

Prepare potato galettes: wash potatoes, wipe dry with a towel, and grate unpeeled potatoes into a colander. Press down on the grated potatoes to release as much water as possible, and then combine them in a bowl with LuLu Basil Pistou and salt and pepper.

In a large sauté pan heat oil over medium-high heat. Using your hands, work quickly to form potato mixture into 4-inch rounds about 1/4-inch thick, and carefully place each round into the hot oil. Fry galettes until golden brown and crispy, approximately 5 minutes on each side. Remove from oil, drain on paper towels and keep warm in a 200° oven.

Prepare chicken: heat grill to medium-high heat. Remove chicken from sauce and grill approximately 5 minutes on each side until cooked through. (Discard bag with remaining sauce.) Remove chicken from grill and season with salt and pepper.

continued

Meanwhile, in a bowl toss salad greens with LuLu Truffle Honey & Meyer Lemon Vinaigrette.

To serve: divide potato galettes and salad greens onto 4 individual plates. Place a chicken breast onto each plate and serve immediately.

Note: We prefer Yukon gold potatoes in this recipe, but you can substitute any type of potato, including the ubiquitous russet. While preparing the galettes, it is important to work quickly or the grated potatoes will turn brown.

Mustard Grilled Veal Chops
with Fingerling Potatoes and Baby Spinach

4 servings

Featuring: **LuLu Mustard with Herbes de Provence**
               LuLu Truffled Artichoke Tapenade

Ingredients: 2 pounds fingerling potatoes
               salt and pepper to taste
               4 tablespoons LuLu Mustard with Herbes de Provence
               6 tablespoons extra virgin olive oil
               4 veal rib chops, about 1-1/2 inches thick
               3 garlic cloves, sliced into thin slivers
               1-1/2 pounds baby spinach leaves
               1 tablespoon chopped fresh thyme
               1 tablespoon chopped fresh parsley
               1 jar LuLu Truffled Artichoke Tapenade

Preparation: Rinse potatoes and pierce all over with a fork. Place in a medium
               saucepan, pour in enough water to cover, add salt, cover saucepan
               and bring to a boil. Reduce heat and cook for 18 to 20 minutes until
               potatoes are fork-tender. Drain potatoes and cut in half lengthwise. Set
               aside.

               Heat grill to medium heat.

               Combine LuLu Mustard with Herbes de Provence with 4 tablespoons of
               the olive oil and rub mixture all over veal chops. Grill veal, flipping chops
               over every 3 to 4 minutes, for a total of about 16 minutes.

               Meanwhile heat remaining 2 tablespoons olive oil in a large sauté pan
               over medium-high heat. Add potatoes cut side down and sprinkle
               with salt and pepper to taste. Cook for 8 minutes until golden brown.
               Stir in garlic and sauté for 2 more minutes. Increase heat to high, add
               baby spinach, cover pan and cook 1 minute to wilt spinach. Remove
               pan from heat and stir in thyme, parsley and LuLu Truffled Artichoke
               Tapenade.

               continued

To serve: place veal chops onto individual plates or a large serving platter, and spoon potato and spinach sauté on the side. Serve immediately.

Note: In this recipe, the grilling time of 16 minutes yields a medium-rare chop. If you prefer your meat more well-done, grill for additional time, continuing to flip chops every 3 to 4 minutes.

Other LuLu Products: If LuLu Mustard with Herbes de Provence is not available, substitute another LuLu Mustard. If LuLu Truffled Artichoke Tapenade is not available, substitute another LuLu Tapenade.

Balsamic Peppercorn Skirt Steak with Grilled Onion Salad

4 servings

Featuring: **LuLu Balsamic Peppercorn Grilling Glaze**
LuLu Fig & Tangerine Balsamic Vinegar

Ingredients:
4 – 8-ounce skirt steaks
1/2 cup plus 2 tablespoons LuLu Balsamic Peppercorn Grilling Glaze
1/2 cup plus 1 tablespoon extra virgin olive oil
salt and pepper to taste
4 tangerines
2 red onions
1 cup LuLu Fig & Tangerine Balsamic Vinegar
4 cups frisée greens (about 3 heads)
4 teaspoons chopped fresh parsley for garnish

Preparation:
Marinate skirt steaks in 1/2 cup LuLu Balsamic Peppercorn Grilling Glaze combined with 1 tablespoon olive oil and salt and pepper for at least 1 hour.

Peel tangerines and cut around membranes into sections. (Cut tangerine sections are known as "supremes".) Set aside. Cut onions into 1-inch thick slices and marinate in 1/2 cup LuLu Fig & Tangerine Balsamic Vinegar while grilling steaks.

Heat grill to high heat.

Remove steaks from Grilling Glaze and grill about 2-1/2 minutes on each side. (Discard excess Glaze.) Remove steaks from grill and cover with foil to keep warm.

Grill onion slices for about 3 minutes on each side until soft. In a large bowl toss onion, frisée and tangerine supremes with remaining 1/2 cup LuLu Fig & Tangerine Balsamic Vinegar, remaining 1/2 cup olive oil and salt and pepper to taste.

continued

To serve: mound salad in the center of a large serving platter or divide onto 4 individual plates. Cut skirt steaks across the grain into 1-inch slices and arrange over salad. Drizzle remaining 2 tablespoons Grilling Glaze over steaks and garnish with parsley.

Note: *Skirt steak is a long thin piece of meat cut from near the cow's rib cage. Its loose grain allows it to absorb lots of flavor when it is marinated. Recently skirt steak has become very popular so unfortunately it can be difficult to find in the market. Some people substitute flank steak for skirt steak, but flank steaks are a tougher cut of meat.*

Other LuLu Products: *If LuLu Balsamic Peppercorn Grilling Glaze is not available, substitute LuLu Pomegranate Grilling Glaze.*

Pan-Seared Chicken with Corn and Peppers

4 servings

Featuring: **LuLu Mustard with Harissa**
              LuLu Heirloom Tomato & Roasted Garlic Sauce

Ingredients: 2 ears of corn, husked
                salt
                4 chicken breast halves (on bone)
                1/2 cup LuLu Mustard with Harissa
                2 tablespoons extra virgin olive oil
                2 bell peppers, assorted colors, cut into julienne slices
                1/2 cup LuLu Heirloom Tomato & Roasted Garlic Sauce
                1/2 cup chicken or vegetable stock or broth
                3 tablespoons chopped fresh parsley

Preparation: Prepare corn: bring a large pot of water to a boil. When water begins
                to boil, add salt and then corn and cook for about 15 minutes. Remove
                corn from pot, cut cobs into 3-inch barrels, set aside and keep warm.

                Meanwhile, place chicken in a shallow bowl and coat with LuLu Mustard
                with Harissa. Heat 1 tablespoon olive oil in a large sauté pan over
                medium-high heat, and sauté chicken for 4 to 5 minutes on each side
                until chicken is golden brown and cooked through. Place chicken on a
                plate and cover with foil to keep warm.

                Wipe sauté pan clean and heat remaining 1 tablespoon olive oil in it.
                Stir in peppers and sauté for 2 to 3 minutes until soft. Stir in LuLu Heirloom
                Tomato & Roasted Garlic Sauce and stock, and simmer sauce for
                5 minutes. Remove from heat and stir in parsley.

                To serve: place chicken on individual plates or a serving platter, and
                arrange corn next to chicken. Spoon sauce over corn and serve
                immediately.

Note: One of the signs that summer has arrived is the appearance of corn in
                the market. If you like sweet corn, find a source close to a farm, because
                once it is harvested the corn's natural sugars convert into starch.

Other LuLu   If LuLu Mustard with Harissa is not available, substitute another LuLu
Products: mustard. If LuLu Heirloom Tomato & Roasted Garlic Sauce is not
                available, substitute LuLu Provençal Roasted Tomato Sauce or LuLu
                Provençal Grilled Vegetable Sauce.

Grilled Meyer Lemon Prawns

4 to 6 servings

Featuring:	**LuLu Preserved Meyer Lemon & Artichoke Vinaigrette** **LuLu Meyer Lemon Marmalade**

Ingredients:

6 cups mixed salad greens
1/3 cup LuLu Preserved Meyer Lemon & Artichoke Vinaigrette
salt and pepper to taste
6 tablespoons LuLu Meyer Lemon Marmalade
3 tablespoons extra virgin olive oil
24 large prawns, peeled and deveined, tails left on
thin slices of Meyer lemon for garnish if desired

Preparation:

Preheat grill to medium-high heat.

In a large bowl toss salad greens with LuLu Preserved Meyer Lemon & Artichoke Vinaigrette. Season with salt and pepper and toss again. Set aside.

In a medium bowl, combine LuLu Meyer Lemon Marmalade with olive oil and brush mixture all over prawns. Season with salt and pepper and grill prawns for 2 minutes on each side.

To serve: mound dressed greens in the center of individual plates or a serving platter, and arrange prawns alongside of salad. Garnish with Meyer lemon slices if desired.

Note: The most common lemon variety found in markets is the Eureka lemon. Meyer lemons, grown primarily in the U.S. in California and Arizona, have a slightly sweeter flavor and a thinner rind which can be eaten as well. LuLu offers several products made from Meyer lemons, including the two used in this recipe.

Other LuLu Products: If LuLu Preserved Meyer Lemon & Artichoke Vinaigrette is not available, substitute LuLu Preserved Meyer Lemon & Olive Vinaigrette. If LuLu Meyer Lemon Marmalade is not available, substitute another LuLu marmalade.

Pomegranate Grilled Pork Chops
with Fennel and Citrus Salad

4 servings

Featuring: **LuLu Pomegranate Grilling Glaze**
LuLu Preserved Meyer Lemon & Artichoke Vinaigrette

Ingredients:
4 pork chops
2 tablespoons extra virgin olive oil
salt and pepper to taste
1/2 pound assorted citrus fruit (see note)
1 fennel bulb
4 radishes
1/2 cup LuLu Pomegranate Grilling Glaze
1 cup mixed salad greens
3 tablespoons LuLu Preserved Meyer Lemon & Artichoke Vinaigrette
pomegranate seeds for garnish if desired

Preparation:
Heat grill to medium heat.

Rinse pork chops and pat dry. Brush chops all over with olive oil, season with salt and pepper and set aside.

Prepare salad ingredients: peel and cut citrus into disks. Cut fennel and radishes into thin slices (preferably with a mandoline). Set aside.

Grill pork chops for about 6 minutes on one side. Turn over and brush the top side with LuLu Pomegranate Grilling Glaze. Grill another 6 minutes or until pork is cooked through. Remove chops from the grill and brush the second side with LuLu Pomegranate Grilling Glaze.

Meanwhile, place prepared citrus, fennel and radishes in a large bowl with mixed salad greens. Toss salad with LuLu Preserved Meyer Lemon & Artichoke Vinaigrette.

To serve: place pork chops onto four individual plates or a platter and arrange salad alongside. Garnish with pomegranate seeds if desired. Serve immediately.

Note: For best results, use at least three different citrus fruits in this recipe; our favorites include Meyer lemons, tangerines, grapefruits and pomelos. You can also substitute red seedless grapes, cut in half, for one of your citrus choices.

Other LuLu Products: If LuLu Pomegranate Grilling Glaze is not available, substitute LuLu Balsamic Peppercorn Grilling Glaze or LuLu Loquat Chili Grilling Glaze. If LuLu Preserved Meyer Lemon & Artichoke Vinaigrette is not available, substitute LuLu Preserved Meyer Lemon & Olive Vinaigrette.

Pan-Seared Duck Breasts
with Braised Artichoke Hearts

6 servings

Featuring: **LuLu Preserved Meyer Lemon & Olive Vinaigrette**
                      LuLu Meyer Lemon & Caramelized Onion Marmalade

Ingredients:

1 lemon, cut in half
6 artichokes
6 boneless duck breasts, skin on and trimmed of excess fat
1/2 cup LuLu Preserved Meyer Lemon & Olive Vinaigrette
2 cups duck or chicken stock
2 cups assorted olives, pitted or unpitted, whole or cut in half
2 tablespoons chopped fresh parsley
2 tablespoons chopped fresh thyme
salt and pepper to taste
6 tablespoons LuLu Meyer Lemon & Caramelized Onion Marmalade
fresh rosemary leaves for garnish

Preparation:

Prepare artichoke hearts: squeeze the juice of half a lemon into a large bowl of cold water. Working with one artichoke at a time and using kitchen gloves to protect your hands, trim outer leaves by peeling them back until they snap off at the base. (You can discard the leaves or save them to make stock.) Using a sharp knife, cut off tops of the inner leaves and cut just a small amount from the stem. Using a paring knife, trim around the edge of the artichoke heart and then scoop out the choke with a spoon. Rub artichoke heart with cut lemon half and place it into the bowl with the lemon water. Repeat with remaining artichokes.

With a sharp knife, score the skin of each duck breast in a 1/2-inch cross-hatch pattern. Heat a large sauté pan over low heat and cook duck breasts, skin-side down, for about 5 to 7 minutes; the duck fat will slowly render during cooking. Pour off accumulated fat into a measuring cup or bowl and set aside. Return pan to low heat and continue cooking for about 5 to 7 more minutes. Turn breasts over and cook for 2 more minutes until meat is cooked through. Remove duck from pan, cover with foil to keep warm, and set aside.

continued

Add 2 tablespoons of the reserved duck fat (or extra virgin olive oil) to sauté pan and increase heat to high. Cut artichoke hearts in quarters and sauté for 2 minutes. Stir in LuLu Preserved Meyer Lemon & Olive Vinaigrette and stock, reduce heat and simmer for 8 to 10 minutes until artichoke hearts have softened. Stir in olives, parsley, thyme and salt and pepper and remove pan from heat.

To serve: remove artichoke hearts and olives from pan with a slotted spoon and arrange on a serving platter or individual plates. Slice duck breasts crosswise on the diagonal and arrange on top of artichokes. Spoon a small amount of braising liquid over each breast and top with a dollop of LuLu Meyer Lemon & Caramelized Onion Marmalade. Garnish with rosemary leaves and serve immediately.

LuLu Balsamic Vinegars

LuLu Grilling Sauces

LuLu Sauces

LuLu Vinaigrettes

LuLu Tapenades

LuLu Mustards

LuLu Mayonnaise

LuLu Sweet & Savory
Complements

LuLu Savory
Complements

LuLu Seasonings

LuLu Marinades

LuLu Sweet
Complements

LuLu Marmalades

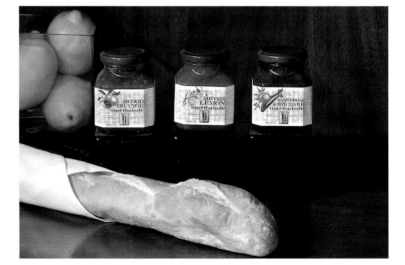

LuLu Jams

From the Oven

Mustard Roasted Rack of Lamb
with Toasted Barley and Ratatouille

4 to 6 servings

Featuring:
LuLu Mustard with Herbes de Provence
LuLu Classic Ratatouille Provençal

Ingredients:
1-1/2 cups pearl barley
2 racks of lamb, about 1-1/2 pounds each
salt and pepper to taste
2 tablespoons extra virgin olive oil
1 sprig fresh rosemary
1 sprig fresh thyme
1 bay leaf
4-1/2 cups chicken or vegetable stock or broth
2 tablespoons LuLu Mustard with Herbes de Provence
1 cup panko (Japanese breadcrumbs)
1 jar LuLu Classic Ratatouille Provençal
2 tablespoons chopped fresh parsley
1 tablespoon chopped fresh thyme

Preparation:
Preheat oven to 400°.

Pour barley in a baking pan and toast in oven for 6 to 8 minutes.

Meanwhile rinse lamb, pat dry, and season with salt and pepper. Using 2 large sauté pans, heat 1 tablespoon olive oil in each pan over medium-high heat. Place a rack of lamb into each sauté pan and quickly sear on all sides. Carefully remove racks from sauté pans and place both into a large roasting pan meaty side down (bones curving upwards). Transfer to oven and roast for about 10 minutes.

When barley has finished toasting, transfer it to a medium saucepan with rosemary and thyme sprigs, and bay leaf. Pour stock over barley and season with salt and pepper. Cover saucepan, bring to a boil, remove cover, reduce heat and simmer for 18 to 20 minutes until barley is tender.

continued

Remove lamb from oven after 10 minutes. Carefully place lamb onto a cutting board and spread LuLu Mustard with Herbes de Provence over meaty side of each rack. Place panko on a large plate and press mustard side of lamb into panko. Return lamb to roasting pan, panko side up, and roast for 12 to 15 more minutes for medium-rare meat. (Roast up to 5 more minutes for more well-done meat.) Remove from oven and let lamb rest for 10 minutes.

When barley has finished cooking, remove from heat and discard sprigs and bay leaf. Stir in LuLu Classic Ratatouille Provençal, chopped parsley and thyme, and salt and pepper.

To serve: slice racks between the bones into chops. Arrange lamb on a serving platter and spoon barley around lamb. Serve immediately.

White Truffle Honey Roasted Chicken with Sun-Dried Tomato Mashed Potatoes

4 servings

Featuring:	**LuLu White Truffle Honey**
	LuLu Sun-Dried Tomato & Porcini Tapenade

Ingredients:

1 whole fryer chicken, 3 to 4 pounds
1 tablespoon chopped fresh thyme
salt and pepper to taste
6 tablespoons plus 1/2 cup extra virgin olive oil
3 sprigs fresh rosemary
3 tablespoons unsalted butter
2 pounds Yukon gold potatoes, peeled
10 garlic cloves, peeled and left whole
1/3 cup LuLu White Truffle Honey
3 tablespoons LuLu Sun-Dried Tomato & Porcini Tapenade

Preparation:

Preheat oven to 450°.

Rinse chicken and pat dry. Using butcher's twine, tie drumsticks together so they lie close to the body. In a small bowl combine thyme, salt and pepper with 3 tablespoons olive oil and rub this mixture all over chicken, inside and out. Tuck a rosemary sprig between each leg and thigh and place the third sprig into the cavity.

Place butter and 3 tablespoons olive oil into a roasting pan large enough to hold the chicken, and place pan in oven about 2 minutes to melt butter. Stir butter and olive oil together, and then place chicken in pan. Roast for 15 minutes, reduce oven temperature to 350°, and roast 15 more minutes. Baste chicken with pan juices every 5 minutes during roasting time.

Meanwhile pierce each potato once with a sharp knife, and place potatoes and garlic into a large stockpot. Cover potatoes with cold water, cover pot, bring to a boil, reduce heat and simmer for 25 to 30 minutes until potatoes are fork-tender.

continued

After chicken has roasted for 30 minutes, remove it from oven and brush LuLu White Truffle Honey all over. Return chicken to oven and continue roasting, basting every 5 minutes, for about 30 more minutes. (Chicken is done when internal temperature reaches 170° and juices run clear.) Cover chicken with foil and let it rest at least 5 minutes before serving.

When potatoes and garlic are fork-tender, drain and pass them through a food mill. (Alternatively, you can mash them by hand.) In a small bowl combine LuLu Sun-Dried Tomato & Porcini Tapenade with remaining 1/2 cup olive oil. Using a spatula, gently fold tapenade mixture into mashed potatoes; don't stir too hard or long or the potatoes will become glutinous and gummy.

Serve chicken with sun-dried tomato mashed potatoes.

Baked Stuffed Swordfish
with Grilled Vegetable Sauce

6 servings

Featuring:	**LuLu Green Olive Tapenade** **LuLu Provençal Grilled Vegetable Sauce**

Ingredients:
6 - 1/2-inch thick swordfish steaks (about 5 inches in diameter)
salt and pepper to taste
3 cups panko (Japanese breadcrumbs)
1/2 jar LuLu Green Olive Tapenade
1 jar LuLu Provençal Grilled Vegetable Sauce
1 teaspoon red chili flakes
2 tablespoons extra virgin olive oil
1 tablespoon chopped fresh oregano
1 tablespoon chopped fresh thyme

Preparation:
Preheat oven to 425°.

Rinse swordfish, pat dry and season with salt and pepper. Pour panko into a medium bowl and stir in LuLu Green Olive Tapenade. Spoon 2 tablespoons of the panko mixture into the center of each swordfish and fold steaks in half over breadcrumbs. Set aside.

In a large, ovenproof sauté pan, heat LuLu Provençal Grilled Vegetable Sauce plus 1/2 jar water over high heat and bring to a boil. Stir in chili flakes. Carefully lay folded swordfish steaks in sauce in a single layer and drizzle olive oil over steaks. When sauce returns to a boil, remove from heat and place into oven.

Baste swordfish with sauce after it has baked for 4 minutes, and then bake an additional 8 to 10 minutes until swordfish is cooked through. Remove from oven.

To serve: using a slotted spoon, lift swordfish from sauté pan and arrange on a serving platter. Spoon sauce over swordfish and sprinkle with oregano and thyme. Serve immediately.

Note: Polenta is a wonderful accompaniment to this recipe. Prepare it according to package directions and serve it warm spooned alongside the swordfish. The flavors in the grilled vegetable sauce will complement the natural sweetness of the polenta.

Other LuLu Products: If LuLu Green Olive Tapenade is not available, substitute another LuLu Tapenade. If LuLu Provençal Grilled Vegetable Sauce is not available, substitute LuLu Provençal Roasted Tomato Sauce or LuLu Heirloom Tomato & Roasted Garlic Sauce.

Preserved Meyer Lemon and Rosemary Roasted Chicken Breasts with Baby Carrots and Wild Rice

6 servings

Featuring: **LuLu Preserved Meyer Lemon & Rosemary Marinade**
LuLu Essence of Orange Blossom Honey

Ingredients:
6 boneless, skinless chicken breasts
1 jar LuLu Preserved Meyer Lemon & Rosemary Marinade
2 tablespoons butter
1 bunch green onions, thinly sliced
2 bunches baby carrots (about 1 pound), trimmed and peeled
1 cup wild rice (uncooked)
2 tablespoons LuLu Essence of Orange Blossom Honey
salt and pepper

Preparation:
Begin marinating chicken breasts at least 1 day in advance (preferably 24 to 36 hours). In a mixing bowl pour LuLu Preserved Meyer Lemon & Rosemary Marinade over chicken breasts and mix together with your hands. Place chicken in a large, sealable plastic bag with all of the marinade. Store refrigerated until ready to cook.

Preheat oven to 350°.

In a medium saucepot heat butter over medium heat. Stir in green onions and cook 2 to 3 minutes until translucent. Stir in baby carrots, wild rice and LuLu Essence of Orange Blossom Honey. Add 4 cups of water, cover pot and cook for 25 minutes. Test rice for doneness; when rice is finished, strain it to remove excess water. Set aside and keep warm.

Meanwhile, remove chicken from plastic bag and discard bag. Place chicken in a single layer in a shallow roasting pan. Sprinkle lightly with salt and pepper and place in oven. Roast for 5 minutes, turn breasts over and roast 5 more minutes until cooked through.

To serve: spoon rice mixture onto a large serving platter. Slice chicken breast crosswise and place on top of rice. Serve immediately.

Note: *The name wild rice is actually a misnomer. Wild rice is technically a long-grain marsh grass. It's known for its nutty flavor and toothsome texture.*

Other LuLu
Products: *If LuLu Preserved Meyer Lemon & Rosemary Marinade is not available, substitute Preserved Meyer Lemon, Fennel & Sage Marinade. If LuLu Essence of Orange Blossom Honey is not available, substitute LuLu Essence of Lavender Honey.*

Meyer Lemon and Sage Roasted Pork Loin with Warm Apple Salad

6 servings

Featuring: **LuLu Preserved Meyer Lemon, Fennel & Sage Marinade**
LuLu Cherry Balsamic Vinegar

Ingredients:
1 boneless pork loin roast, about 3-1/2 pounds
1 jar LuLu Preserved Meyer Lemon, Fennel & Sage Marinade
salt and pepper to taste
1 bunch watercress
2 pounds Fuji apples (or your favorite variety)
1 tablespoon butter
1 tablespoon extra virgin olive oil
1 tablespoon sugar
1/2 cup currants
1/2 cup LuLu Cherry Balsamic Vinegar

Preparation:
Marinate pork: 24 to 36 hours in advance, rinse and pat dry pork loin and place in a large mixing bowl. Spoon LuLu Preserved Meyer Lemon, Fennel & Sage Marinade onto pork and rub all over with your hands. Place pork in a sealable plastic bag and refrigerate until ready to roast.

Preheat oven to 350°.

Remove pork from plastic bag and discard bag. Season pork with salt and pepper and place in a roasting pan. Roast in oven (or on a rotisserie) for approximately 1 hour or until pork reaches an internal temperature of 145°. Remove from oven, cover with foil and let pork rest for at least 10 minutes. (Internal temperature will increase while pork is resting.)

Rinse and dry watercress, remove tough stems and set aside. Remove cores from apples and cut each into 6 wedges. In a sauté pan over high heat, brown butter. Stir in extra virgin olive oil and then stir in apple wedges. Sauté apples for 2 minutes, sprinkle sugar on them and continue cooking for 2 more minutes. Stir in currants and LuLu Cherry Balsamic Vinegar and continue cooking for 3 minutes to glaze apples.

continued

To serve: arrange watercress on a large platter, and spoon warm apple salad on top of watercress. Slice pork loin into 1-inch thick slices and arrange over apple salad. Serve immediately.

Note:

There are thousands of varieties of apples that grow throughout the world. Available year-round, apples are at their most flavorful during the autumn harvest. For this recipe choose a firm, crisp variety (any color) so the apples won't become mushy during cooking.

Lavender Honey Glazed Duck with Red Plum Glazed Figs

4 to 6 servings

Featuring:
LuLu Sage Roasted Meat Seasoning
LuLu Essence of Lavender Honey
LuLu Red Plum & Roasted Onion Conserve

Ingredients:
2 whole ducks, about 5 pounds each
3 tablespoons LuLu Sage Roasted Meat Seasoning
1 jar LuLu Essence of Lavender Honey
1 jar LuLu Red Plum & Roasted Onion Conserve
1/4 cup duck or chicken stock
1 pint fresh figs, stemmed and cut into quarters
2 tablespoons chopped fresh parsley
2 tablespoons chopped fresh thyme

Preparation:
One day in advance, rinse and pat dry ducks and season inside and out with LuLu Sage Roasted Meat Seasoning. Place in a large, sealable plastic bag and refrigerate overnight.

Preheat oven to 325°.

Remove ducks from plastic bag and discard bag. Using a sharp knife or skewer, prick the skin of the duck all over (this will allow the fat to drain and skin to crisp while roasting). Place ducks on a rack in a roasting pan and roast for 45 minutes. Remove ducks from oven and brush all over with LuLu Essence of Lavender Honey. Return ducks to oven and continue roasting for an additional 45 minutes, basting with the honey every 15 minutes, until skin is brown and ducks reach an internal temperature of 175°. Remove ducks from oven, cover with foil, and let them rest for at least 5 minutes.

Meanwhile combine LuLu Red Plum & Roasted Onion Conserve and stock in a sauté pan over medium heat. Bring mixture to a simmer and remove from heat. Stir in figs and let them steep for 5 minutes. Stir in parsley and thyme.

continued

To serve: place ducks, either whole or cut into serving pieces, onto a large platter and spoon figs around ducks. Serve immediately.

Note: The most common type of duck available is the Long Island duck, which was originally bred from ducks brought to the U.S. from China. If your duck is frozen, you will need to thaw it in the refrigerator for 24 to 36 hours before marinating it overnight, so plan accordingly.

Other LuLu Products: If LuLu Sage Roasted Meat Seasoning is not available, substitute another LuLu Seasoning. If LuLu Red Plum & Roasted Onion Conserve is not available, substitute LuLu Loquat Mint Jam with Currants or LuLu Meyer Lemon & Caramelized Onion Marmalade.

Baked Halibut Steaks
with Preserved Meyer Lemon

4 to 6 servings

Featuring: **LuLu Preserved Meyer Lemon in Olive Oil**
LuLu Preserved Meyer Lemon & Rosemary Marinade
LuLu Sun-Dried Tomato & Porcini Tapenade

Ingredients: 1/3 cup LuLu Preserved Meyer Lemon in Olive Oil
2 pounds halibut steaks or fillets (4 to 6 pieces)
salt and pepper to taste
1/2 cup vegetable stock or broth
2 bunches asparagus, trimmed
1/2 cup LuLu Preserved Meyer Lemon & Rosemary Marinade
1/4 cup extra virgin olive oil
4 ounces (1 stick) butter, cut into 8 pieces
2 tablespoons minced chives
4 to 6 tablespoons LuLu Sun-Dried Tomato & Porcini Tapenade
2 tablespoons chopped fresh basil

Preparation: Preheat oven to 425° and heat grill to medium-high heat.

Spread LuLu Preserved Meyer Lemon in Olive Oil all over halibut and season lightly with salt and pepper. Pour stock into a roasting pan, lay halibut in pan in a single layer, and place pan in oven. Bake 8 to 10 minutes until halibut is cooked through.

Meanwhile blanch asparagus in boiling water for 4 minutes and immediately plunge it into an ice bath. In a large bowl combine LuLu Preserved Meyer Lemon & Rosemary Marinade and olive oil. Drain asparagus and toss it with mixture in bowl. Grill asparagus for about 4 minutes until browned, remove from heat, and set aside.

When halibut has finished baking prepare beurre blanc: remove halibut from roasting pan and cover with foil to keep warm. Place roasting pan on stovetop over high heat and bring stock to a boil. Reduce heat to a simmer and whisk in one piece of butter; when butter has melted whisk in second piece. Repeat until all of the butter has been blended into stock. Remove from heat.

continued

To serve: divide asparagus among individual plates, spoon beurre blanc over asparagus and sprinkle with chives. Place halibut atop asparagus and top it with a dollop of LuLu Sun-Dried Tomato & Porcini Tapenade and a sprinkle of basil. Serve immediately.

Note: *Occasionally pencil-thin asparagus is available in markets. In general, thin asparagus is sweeter and more tender than thicker asparagus, and cooks in less time. If you use it in this recipe, omit the blanching and ice bath steps, and proceed to tossing it with the marinade mixture and grilling it.*

Mustard Roasted Turkey with Savory Gravy

8 to 10 servings

Featuring: **LuLu Mustard with Preserved Lemon & Garlic**

Ingredients: 1 small turkey (up to 12 pounds)
1 jar LuLu Mustard with Preserved Lemon & Garlic
1 tablespoon sea salt plus more to taste
1/4 cup extra virgin olive oil
1 carrot, chopped
1 onion, peeled and chopped
1 stalk celery, chopped
1-1/2 cups white wine
1 clove garlic, peeled and sliced
1 bay leaf
1 teaspoon whole black peppercorns
2 quarts chicken stock or broth, or water
1-1/2 tablespoons flour
2 tablespoons butter
pepper to taste

Preparation: Two days in advance remove neck and giblets from inside turkey and set aside. Rinse turkey and pat dry. In a small bowl whisk together LuLu Mustard with Preserved Lemon & Garlic, sea salt and olive oil and rub mixture all over turkey, inside and out, as well as on the neck and giblets. Place turkey breast-side down into a large container, cover and store in the refrigerator. Place neck and giblets in a sealable plastic bag and refrigerate.

One day in advance prepare turkey stock: preheat oven to 350°. Place neck and giblets in a roasting pan along with carrot, onion and celery, and roast for about 1 hour until well-browned. Place roasted neck, giblets and vegetables in a saucepot. Deglaze roasting pan with wine and add to large saucepot along with garlic, bay leaf, peppercorns and a pinch of salt. Pour in stock; make sure liquid covers solids by 2 inches.

Heat saucepot over high heat for about 10 minutes but do not boil. After 10 minutes reduce heat to the lowest setting and simmer for 6 to 8 hours, adding stock or water if more liquid is needed.

continued

Strain stock, discard solids and allow stock to cool to room temperature. Refrigerate turkey stock overnight.

Four hours in advance preheat oven to 450°. Place turkey in a roasting pan and roast for 15 minutes. Reduce oven temperature to 250° and continue roasting turkey for about 3 hours; turkey is done when internal temperature reaches 155°. Remove turkey from roasting pan and place on a large platter to collect juices. Cover it with foil and allow it to rest for 30 to 45 minutes before serving. (Internal temperature will continue to rise while turkey is resting.)

continued

While turkey is resting prepare gravy: remove turkey stock from refrigerator, discard congealed fat from surface and heat stock. Heat turkey roasting pan over medium heat and vigorously whisk in flour. Continue whisking for 3 minutes until flour begins to brown. Whisk in 1 cup heated turkey stock and cook, whisking continuously, for about 10 minutes; gravy should begin to thicken. (Add more stock if gravy becomes too thick.) Simmer gravy for about 20 minutes, then stir in accumulated juices from the turkey platter along with butter. Taste gravy and adjust salt and pepper if desired.

Carve turkey and serve with gravy.

Note:

Most people serve roast turkey for the holidays, but it is an easy way to feed a crowd any time of the year! We prefer a small turkey, which will roast more evenly than a large one, however this recipe can be adjusted for a larger turkey by increasing the amount of LuLu Mustard and increasing the cooking time. We recommend serving the Butternut Squash and Potato Gratin (page 142) as an accompaniment to this recipe.

Other LuLu Products:

If LuLu Mustard with Preserved Lemon & Garlic is not available, substitute another LuLu Mustard.

Vegetables

Sautéed Asparagus
with Radishes and Preserved Lemon
4 to 6 servings

Featuring: **LuLu Preserved Meyer Lemon in Olive Oil**

Ingredients:
2 bunches asparagus, trimmed
5 tablespoons extra virgin olive oil
1 bunch French Breakfast radishes, trimmed and cut in half lengthwise
salt and pepper to taste
2 tablespoons LuLu Preserved Meyer Lemon in Olive Oil
1 tablespoon chopped fresh thyme
1 tablespoon chopped fresh parsley

Preparation:
Bring a large pot of water to a boil. Blanch asparagus in boiling water for 4 minutes and immediately plunge it into an ice bath. (If using pencil-thin asparagus, you can omit the blanching and cooling steps.) When cool, cut asparagus into 2-inch pieces and set aside.

Heat 2 tablespoons olive oil in a large sauté pan over high heat. Stir in radishes and sauté for 3 minutes. Season with salt and pepper.

Add 2 more tablespoons olive oil to sauté pan and stir in asparagus pieces and LuLu Preserved Meyer Lemon in Olive Oil. Sauté for 3 more minutes and then stir in thyme and parsley. Remove from heat.

To serve: arrange vegetables on a serving platter and drizzle with remaining tablespoon olive oil. Serve warm or at room temperature.

Note: *French Breakfast radishes, also known as Flambo, have an elongated shape and range in color from white to pink to red. If this type of radish is not available, you can substitute any other type of radish, including the popular Red Globe variety.*

Grilled Vegetables with Mustard Dressing

4 to 6 servings

Featuring: **LuLu Mustard with Harissa**

Ingredients:
4 Japanese eggplants, trimmed and cut in half lengthwise
2 yellow sunburst squash, trimmed and cut into quarters
4 zucchini, trimmed and cut into quarters lengthwise
2 bunches green onions, ends trimmed
2 red bell peppers
2 Italian frying peppers or 1 green bell pepper
2 pasilla chile peppers
2 gypsy peppers
3/4 cup extra virgin olive oil
salt and pepper to taste
4 tablespoons LuLu Mustard with Harissa
2 tablespoons chopped fresh oregano
2 tablespoons chopped fresh parsley
1 teaspoon chopped fresh thyme

Preparation:
Heat grill to high heat.

In a large bowl, toss eggplant, squash, zucchini, green onions and all of the peppers with 1/2 cup olive oil, salt and pepper. Grill for 4 to 5 minutes, turning vegetables every minute until all are evenly browned. Remove from heat; place eggplant, squash and green onions in a clean, large bowl and place all peppers on a cutting board.

Using a sharp paring knife, cut stems from all peppers. Leaving bell peppers whole, remove their seeds and membranes. Add all peppers to bowl with other vegetables.

In a small bowl whisk together LuLu Mustard with Harissa, remaining olive oil, oregano, parsley and thyme. Toss vegetables with mustard mixture, taste and adjust salt and pepper.

To serve: arrange vegetables on a large platter. Serve warm or at room temperature.

Note: The method in this recipe will work with an assortment of vegetables, so
                   feel free to substitute from whatever is available in your market. For the
                   squash and zucchini choose any summer squash, and for the peppers
                   choose from a range of flavors (sweet to hot) and colors.

Other LuLu   If LuLu Mustard with Harissa is not available, substitute another LuLu
Products: Mustard.

Fire-Roasted Corn on the Cob

6 servings

Featuring:	**LuLu Sun-Dried Tomato & Porcini Tapenade**
Ingredients:	6 ears of corn (with husks on)
	1/2 jar LuLu Sun-Dried Tomato & Porcini Tapenade
	4 tablespoons unsalted butter, cut into 4 pieces
	1 tablespoon fresh Italian parsley leaves
	salt and pepper to taste
Preparation:	Heat grill to medium-high heat.

Remove outside layers of corn husks except for 2 of the inner layers. Carefully peel back the inner husks about three-quarters of the way down the corn cob and remove the corn silk. Replace the inner husk around the corn cob and grill corn, turning every 5 minutes, for about 15 minutes until husks are blackened. Remove from grill.

While corn is grilling, combine LuLu Sun-Dried Tomato & Porcini Tapenade and 2 tablespoons water in a small saucepan and warm over medium-low heat for about 4 minutes. Remove from heat and stir in butter; butter should not melt completely.

To serve: peel back husks from ears of corn but leave husk attached at the base. Arrange corn on a platter and spread tapenade mixture all over corn. Garnish with parsley leaves and serve immediately.

Note: *Here's an interesting food trivia fact: each kernel of corn begins its life as a corn silk. That means that there are exactly the same number of silk strands on an ear of corn as there are kernels.*

Other LuLu Products: *If LuLu Sun-Dried Tomato & Porcini Tapenade is not available, substitute LuLu Romesco Sauce or LuLu Roasted Tomato Harissa.*

Balsamic Peppercorn Grilled Bell Peppers

4 servings

Featuring: **LuLu Balsamic Peppercorn Grilling Glaze**

Ingredients:
2 red bell peppers
2 yellow bell peppers
1 tablespoon extra virgin olive oil
3 tablespoons LuLu Balsamic Peppercorn Grilling Glaze
2 sprigs fresh rosemary

Preparation: Heat grill to medium-high heat.

Place peppers in a large bowl and toss with extra virgin olive oil and 2 tablespoons LuLu Balsamic Peppercorn Grilling Glaze. Grill peppers for about 2 minutes on each of 4 sides until lightly browned all over. Remove from grill.

To serve: arrange peppers in a serving bowl and drizzle with remaining LuLu Balsamic Peppercorn Grilling Glaze. Garnish with rosemary sprigs and serve warm or at room temperature.

Note: Alternatively, you can serve the bell peppers cut into pieces instead of whole. Using a sharp paring knife, cut stems and remove seeds and membranes. Cut peppers into quarters or thin slices and arrange on a serving platter and drizzle with the grilling glaze. These peppers are a delicious accompaniment to grilled steaks and pork.

Other LuLu Products: If LuLu Balsamic Peppercorn Grilling Glaze is not available, substitute LuLu Pomegranate Grilling Glaze or LuLu Sweet & Spicy Tomato Grilling Glaze.

Sautéed Summer Beans with Almonds

6 servings

Featuring: **LuLu Roasted Tomato Harissa**

Ingredients: 2 cups green string beans
2 cups yellow wax beans
2 cups Romano (Italian flat) beans
2 tablespoons extra virgin olive oil
1-1/2 teaspoons chopped garlic
salt and pepper to taste
6 tablespoons LuLu Roasted Tomato Harissa
1/3 cup slivered almonds, toasted

Preparation: Bring a large pot of water to a boil. Blanch green beans in boiling water for 4 minutes and immediately plunge them into an ice bath. Repeat blanching and cooling with yellow wax beans, then Romano beans. When all the beans have cooled, drain them and set aside.

Heat olive oil in a large sauté pan over high heat. Stir in cooled beans and sauté for 3 minutes. Stir in garlic and continue to sauté for 3 more minutes. Remove from heat and stir in LuLu Roasted Tomato Harissa, and salt and pepper to taste.

To serve: spoon beans into a large bowl or platter and top with toasted slivered almonds. Serve immediately.

Note: The name summer beans refers to fresh beans as opposed to dried
                   beans. Although most fresh beans are still in their pods, the term also
                   includes fava beans which are shelled before eating. This recipe can be
                   prepared with any combination of summer beans in pods, also known as
                   snap beans.

Other LuLu   If LuLu Roasted Tomato Harissa is not available, substitute LuLu Romesco
Products: Sauce.

Braised Fennel and Red Onion with Figs

4 to 6 servings

Featuring: **LuLu Fig & Meyer Lemon Balsamic Vinegar**

Ingredients: 2 fennel bulbs
1 large red onion
1/4 cup extra virgin olive oil
1/4 cup LuLu Fig & Meyer Lemon Balsamic Vinegar
1/2 cup vegetable stock or broth
6 sprigs fresh thyme
1 bay leaf
1/2 pound fresh figs, trimmed and cut into quarters
2 tablespoons unsalted butter
2 tablespoons chopped fresh parsley

Preparation: Preheat oven to 425°.

Trim fennel bulbs: cut a small slice from the bottom (root end) and remove the tops and fronds (feathery leaves). Cut each bulb in half lengthwise, and then cut each half into 3 or 4 wedges. Cut onion into 1/2-inch slices.

In a large ovenproof sauté pan, heat olive oil over high heat. Cook fennel and onion for about 6 minutes, turning pieces once during cooking, until vegetables have caramelized. Stir in LuLu Fig & Meyer Lemon Balsamic Vinegar, stock, thyme sprigs and bay leaf and bring to a boil. Remove from heat.

Place pan in oven and braise vegetables for about 10 minutes until fennel bulbs have softened. Remove pan from oven. Gently stir in figs and butter.

To serve: spoon vegetables, figs and braising liquid into a serving bowl or platter, and top with chopped parsley. Serve immediately.

Note: *Fresh fennel bulbs, also known as finocchio, are sometimes sold as fresh anise in stores due to its slight licorice flavor. Both fennel and fresh figs are at their peak during the autumn months. This recipe is a flavorful accompaniment to roast pork and lamb.*

Other LuLu Products: *If LuLu Fig & Meyer Lemon Balsamic Vinegar is not available, substitute another LuLu Balsamic Vinegar.*

Roasted Cauliflower with Olive Tapenade

4 to 6 servings

Featuring:	**LuLu Olive Tapenade**

Ingredients:

2 heads cauliflower, cored and cut into 2-inch florets
1/4 cup plus 1 tablespoon extra virgin olive oil
3 tablespoons LuLu Olive Tapenade
4 sprigs fresh rosemary
salt and pepper to taste

Preparation:

Preheat oven to 425°.

In a large ovenproof sauté pan heat 1/4 cup olive oil over high heat. Stir in cauliflower and sauté for 3 minutes until cauliflower begins to brown. Place pan in oven and roast cauliflower for about 12 minutes, stirring every 4 minutes, until evenly browned. Remove pan from oven and stir in LuLu Olive Tapenade, remaining olive oil, rosemary sprigs, and salt and pepper.

To serve: arrange cauliflower on a serving platter and serve immediately.

Note:	Cauliflower is a nutritious and versatile vegetable that lends itself to many different preparations, such as steaming, boiling, and sautéing. In this easy recipe, roasting the cauliflower mellows its strong flavor.
Other LuLu Products:	If LuLu Olive Tapenade is not available, substitute another LuLu Tapenade.

Fingerling Potatoes
with Wild Mushrooms and Dandelion Greens

4 to 6 servings

Featuring:
LuLu Herbes de Provence Seasoning
LuLu Mustard with Preserved Lemon & Garlic

Ingredients:
1 pound fingerling or yellow Finn potatoes, cut into 1/4-inch thick slices
2 tablespoons extra virgin olive oil
1 teaspoon LuLu Herbes de Provence Seasoning
salt and pepper to taste
1 pound specialty mushrooms, such as portobella, morels or chanterelles
1/4 cup LuLu Mustard with Preserved Lemon & Garlic
1 cup baby dandelion greens, watercress or arugula
1 tablespoon white truffle oil
1/4 cup thinly-shaved Parmesan cheese

Preparation:
Preheat oven to 350°.

In a medium bowl, toss potato slices with 1 tablespoon olive oil,
1/2 teaspoon LuLu Herbes de Provence Seasoning, salt and pepper.
Spread potatoes evenly on a baking sheet and sprinkle with
2 tablespoons water. Roast potatoes in oven 30 to 40 minutes until
fork-tender. Remove from oven and set aside.

Meanwhile, clean mushrooms and trim any hard stems. If mushrooms are
small leave them whole; halve, quarter or chop any large mushrooms.
In a large bowl, toss mushrooms with 1 tablespoon olive oil, 1/2
teaspoon LuLu Herbes de Provence Seasoning, salt and pepper. Spread
mushrooms evenly on a baking sheet and roast for 10 minutes. Remove
from oven and set aside.

Heat a large sauté pan over high heat. Stir in roasted potatoes and
mushrooms and sauté for 3 minutes until heated through. Remove pan
from heat and stir in LuLu Mustard with Preserved Lemon & Garlic. Spoon
potato and mushroom mixture into a large bowl and gently toss with
dandelion greens. Season with salt and pepper to taste.

continued

To serve: arrange potato mixture on a serving platter. Drizzle with white truffle oil and top with Parmesan cheese. Serve immediately.

Note: *Mushrooms can be cleaned by gently removing dirt with a mushroom brush, wiping them with a dry paper towel, or shaking them in a colander under running water. In this recipe when the mushrooms are roasting they will release water, however they will cook more evenly if they are as dry as possible prior to roasting.*

Other LuLu Products: *If LuLu Mustard with Preserved Lemon & Garlic is not available, substitute another LuLu Mustard.*

Roasted Acorn Squash, Potatoes and Pears with Gorgonzola

4 to 6 servings

Featuring: **LuLu Fig Balsamic Vinegar**

Ingredients:
1 acorn squash, cut into 8 wedges, seeds removed and peeled if desired
1 pound fingerling or other small potato
1 pound cipollini or other small onion
1/2 cup extra virgin olive oil
1/3 cup plus 2 tablespoons LuLu Fig Balsamic Vinegar
salt and pepper to taste
3 pears, cored and cut into wedges
4 sprigs fresh thyme
1/2 cup Gorgonzola cheese
1/4 cup chopped, toasted hazelnuts

Preparation: Preheat oven to 400°.

In a large mixing bowl, toss acorn squash, potatoes and onions with olive oil, 1/3 cup LuLu Fig Balsamic Vinegar and a little salt and pepper. Spread vegetables evenly on a baking sheet or shallow roasting pan and roast for 20 minutes, stirring every 5 minutes. Remove from oven.

Sprinkle pears and thyme with salt and pepper and arrange evenly over vegetables. Return to oven for 10 more minutes.

To serve: arrange vegetables on a large platter, drizzle with remaining LuLu Fig Balsamic Vinegar and crumble Gorgonzola cheese over the top. Sprinkle with hazelnuts and serve immediately.

Note: *In this recipe you can substitute other winter squashes (butternut, kabocha, turban) and even pumpkin for the acorn squash – be sure to cut whichever squash you choose into large, uniform pieces before baking.*

Other LuLu Products: *If LuLu Fig Balsamic Vinegar is not available, substitute another LuLu Balsamic Vinegar.*

Meyer Lemon and Rosemary Roasted Potatoes

4 to 6 servings

Featuring: **LuLu Preserved Meyer Lemon & Rosemary Marinade**

Ingredients:
1 pound fingerling or other small potato
1 pound cipollini or other small onion
4 tablespoons LuLu Preserved Meyer Lemon & Rosemary Marinade
3 tablespoons extra virgin olive oil
salt and pepper to taste
1 cup baby spinach leaves

Preparation:
Preheat oven to 450°.

Remove any dirt from potatoes and cut in half lengthwise. In a medium bowl, toss potatoes with 2 tablespoons LuLu Preserved Meyer Lemon & Rosemary Marinade, 2 tablespoons olive oil, salt and pepper. Spread evenly on a baking sheet and roast for 5 minutes.

Meanwhile, in a separate bowl toss onions with remaining LuLu Preserved Meyer Lemon & Rosemary Marinade, salt and pepper and set aside.

After potatoes have roasted for 5 minutes, add onions to baking sheet and drizzle with remaining olive oil. Roast for about 15 more minutes until potatoes are golden-brown and fork-tender. Remove from oven.

To serve: spoon potatoes and onions into a serving bowl and gently toss with spinach (the heat will wilt the spinach). Serve immediately.

Note: Fingerlings are similar to russet potatoes, except they have thinner skins and are smaller in size. The name refers to their shape, which resembles large fingers. If fingerling potatoes are not available, use another type of small potato (Yukon gold, or red or white new potatoes), or use russets that have been cut into 2-inch pieces.

Other LuLu Products: If LuLu Preserved Meyer Lemon & Rosemary Marinade is not available, substitute LuLu Preserved Meyer Lemon, Fennel & Sage Marinade.

Truffled Artichoke Mashed Potatoes

6 to 8 servings

Featuring: **LuLu Truffled Artichoke Tapenade**

Ingredients: 4 pounds Yukon gold potatoes, peeled
                6 garlic cloves, peeled and left whole
                salt to taste
                1 cup heavy whipping cream or milk
                1/2 jar LuLu Truffled Artichoke Tapenade
                pepper to taste

Preparation: Place potatoes and garlic cloves in a large stockpot, cover with cold
                water, add salt, cover pot, bring to a boil, reduce heat and simmer for
                25 to 30 minutes until potatoes are fork-tender.

                Remove pot from heat, drain and pass potato and garlic through a food
                mill. (Alternatively, you can mash them by hand.) Stir in cream until just
                combined. Using a spatula, gently fold LuLu Truffled Artichoke Tapenade
                into mashed potatoes; don't stir too hard or too long or the mashed
                potatoes will become glutinous and gummy. Taste and adjust salt and
                pepper.

                To serve: spoon into a serving bowl or onto individual plates and serve
                immediately.

| Note: | We are big fans of Yukon gold potatoes, with their yellow-gold flesh and thin skins. Yukon golds have a higher moisture content and contain less starch, which is perfect for light and fluffy mashed potatoes. If Yukon gold potatoes are not available, you can substitute any other type of potato. |

| Other LuLu Products: | If LuLu Truffled Artichoke Tapenade is not available, substitute another LuLu Tapenade. |

Fennel and Lemon-Scented Rice

6 to 8 servings

Featuring: **LuLu Preserved Meyer Lemon, Fennel & Sage Marinade**

Ingredients: 3 cups long-grain white rice
                 6 cups water
                 1/2 jar LuLu Preserved Meyer Lemon, Fennel & Sage Marinade
                 salt and pepper to taste
                 3 tablespoons unsalted butter
                 3 tablespoons chopped fresh parsley

Preparation: In a large saucepot combine rice, water, LuLu Preserved Meyer Lemon,
                 Fennel & Sage Marinade, salt and pepper. Bring to a boil, reduce heat
                 and simmer for 18 to 20 minutes until rice is tender.

                 Remove from heat and fluff rice with a fork. Stir in butter and parsley.
                 Spoon into a serving bowl and serve immediately.

Note:	You can substitute brown rice for white rice in this recipe, however you will need to adjust the amount of water used and cooking time. Use the package directions on the brown rice as your guide.
Other LuLu Products:	If LuLu Preserved Meyer Lemon, Fennel & Sage Marinade is not available, substitute LuLu Preserved Meyer Lemon & Rosemary Marinade.

Butternut Squash and Potato Gratin

8 to 10 servings

Featuring:	**LuLu Au Poivre Marinade**

Ingredients:
2 butternut squash
4 russet potatoes
salt to taste
4 cups heavy whipping cream
3 tablespoons LuLu Au Poivre Marinade
3 tablespoons chopped fresh thyme
1 cup freshly grated Parmesan cheese
1 cup panko (Japanese breadcrumbs)
2 tablespoons chopped fresh parsley for garnish

Preparation:

Preheat oven to 375°.

Peel and seed squash and cut into thin (1/8-inch) slices. Peel and cut potatoes into thin (1/8-inch) slices. Place squash and potato slices into a large bowl, season with salt and stir in cream, LuLu Au Poivre Marinade and thyme. Using a slotted spoon, layer squash and potato slices evenly into a 9- by 13-inch baking dish and then pour cream mixture over vegetables. Bake gratin for 1 hour and 15 minutes until vegetables are fork-tender. (Do not stir during baking.)

Top with Parmesan cheese and panko and bake for 10 more minutes until top is golden-brown. Remove from oven.

To serve: sprinkle with parsley and serve immediately.

Note:	This recipe can be prepared in advance by allowing the gratin to cool after its initial baking time (1 hour and 15 minutes). Once gratin has cooled, cover and refrigerate it. Before serving, warm gratin for 15 minutes at 375°, then finish recipe by topping gratin with Parmesan cheese and panko and baking for the additional 10 minutes. This recipe is a wonderful accompaniment to Mustard Roasted Turkey (page 112), and preparing it in advance makes it perfect for the busy holiday season.
Other LuLu Products:	If LuLu Au Poivre Marinade is not available, substitute another LuLu Marinade.

Desserts

Fresh Berries
with Orange Blossom Honey Sabayon
6 to 8 servings

Featuring: **LuLu Essence of Orange Blossom Honey**

Ingredients: 16 egg yolks
                  1 cup sugar
                  1/2 cup LuLu Essence of Orange Blossom Honey
                  2 tablespoons freshly-squeezed lemon juice
                  12 tablespoons (1-1/2 sticks) unsalted butter at room temperature
                  8 ounces fresh raspberries
                  6 ounces fresh blueberries
                  6 ounces fresh blackberries
                  about 15 fresh mint leaves

Preparation: Prepare sabayon: in a large stainless steel bowl, whisk together egg
                  yolks, sugar, LuLu Essence of Orange Blossom Honey and lemon juice.
                  Set bowl in a bain marie (see note), and whisk continuously until mixture
                  begins to thicken. (Test mixture by "drawing" a figure eight in it with a
                  knife; it should hold its shape for 2 to 3 seconds.)

                  Remove bowl from bain marie and whisk in butter, 1 tablespoon at a
                  time, until all of the butter is blended into sabayon. Set aside.

                  In a separate medium bowl, gently toss berries together. Chiffonade
                  mint leaves by slicing them into very thin strips; do not chop mint leaves.

                  To serve: divide berries into individual bowls or wine glasses and spoon
                  sabayon over them. Top with mint chiffonade and serve immediately.

Note: Bain marie refers to a French cooking technique that uses a warm water bath to gently cook delicate foods. To prepare a bain marie, pour 2 to 3 inches of hot water into a shallow pan, then set the bowl containing your ingredients into the "bath". In this recipe the heat of the warm water will cook the egg yolks without curdling them.

An easy way to chiffonade herbs is to stack the leaves on top of one another, then gently roll leaves into a cylinder and slice across the leaves. The leaves will darken around each cut line, so it is important to slice in one direction and not to chop.

Other LuLu Products: If LuLu Essence of Orange Blossom Honey is not available, substitute LuLu Essence of Lavender Honey.

Meyer Lemon Ice Cream with Huckleberry Sauce

8 servings

Featuring: **LuLu Meyer Lemon Marmalade**

Ingredients:
2-1/2 cups heavy whipping cream
1-1/4 cups whole milk
1/2 jar LuLu Meyer Lemon Marmalade
4 tablespoons fresh lemon juice, preferably from Meyer lemons
7 egg yolks
3/4 cup sugar
1/2 teaspoon salt
1-1/2 cups huckleberries
fresh mint sprigs for garnish

Preparation:
In a saucepot with a heavy bottom, heat cream, milk, LuLu Meyer Lemon Marmalade and 1 tablespoon lemon juice over high heat until bubbles begin to break the surface; do not boil. Remove from heat and set aside to cool.

In a large bowl, whisk together egg yolks, 1/2 cup sugar and salt. Temper egg mixture by whisking 1 tablespoon of the cream mixture into it, then whisk remaining cream mixture into egg mixture. Cool mixture (custard) in an ice water bath, then cover and refrigerate for at least 2 hours, preferably overnight.

Remove custard from refrigerator, pour into an ice cream maker and prepare according to manufacturer's instructions. Cover and freeze ice cream until ready to serve.

Prepare huckleberry sauce: in a small saucepot heat 1 cup huckleberries, remaining sugar and remaining lemon juice over medium heat for 8 to 10 minutes until berries become juicy. Stir in remaining huckleberries and cook for 2 more minutes. Remove from heat and refrigerate.

To assemble: spoon 2 tablespoons huckleberry sauce into a martini glass or small bowl. Top with 1 scoop Meyer lemon ice cream, drizzle with 2 teaspoons huckleberry sauce, and garnish with mint sprigs. Repeat with remaining huckleberry sauce and ice cream and serve.

| Note: | Huckleberries, which closely resemble blueberries, are not commercially grown so they can only be found in farmers markets and in the wild during the summer months. If you aren't lucky enough to have a huckleberry bush nearby, you can use blueberries or other berries to make the sauce in this recipe. |
| Other LuLu Products: | If LuLu Meyer Lemon Marmalade is not available, substitute another LuLu Marmalade. |

Lavender Honey Panna Cotta

8 servings

Featuring: **LuLu Essence of Lavender Honey**

Ingredients:

2 envelopes unflavored gelatin
2-1/4 cups buttermilk
2 vanilla beans
2-1/4 cups heavy whipping cream
1/3 cup sugar
1/2 cup LuLu Essence of Lavender Honey
2 cups fresh strawberries, stemmed and cut into quarters
fresh mint sprigs for garnish

Preparation:

In a medium bowl, sprinkle gelatin over buttermilk and allow gelatin to soften.

Cut vanilla beans in half lengthwise and scrape out seeds. In a large saucepan combine cream, sugar, 1/4 cup LuLu Essence of Lavender Honey, vanilla beans and seeds and cook over high heat until mixture comes to a boil. Immediately remove from heat.

Whisk buttermilk mixture into saucepan and then pour through a strainer into a large liquid measuring cup (at least 6 cups) or pitcher. Divide into six 6-ounce ramekins or similar molds and refrigerate for at least 6 hours.

To serve: in a small bowl combine strawberries with remaining LuLu Essence of Lavender Honey. Unmold panna cotta: dip bottoms of ramekins into a small bowl of hot water, cut around the inside edges of ramekins with a thin knife, and invert panna cotta onto individual plates. Surround panna cotta with strawberries and garnish with mint sprigs.

Note: You don't have to purchase ramekins to prepare this dessert; there
               are kitchen items that can replace the ramekins. Try using small water
               glasses, teacups, cappuccino cups or even a popover pan!

Other LuLu   If LuLu Essence of Lavender Honey is not available, substitute LuLu
Products: Essence of Orange Blossom Honey.

Bing Cherry Wine Sauce with Vanilla Ice Cream

6 to 8 servings

Featuring: **LuLu Fig Cherry & Balsamic Jam**

Ingredients: 2 pounds fresh Bing cherries, pitted and cut in half
1 lemon, juiced
1 bottle (750 ml) red wine, preferably Pinot Noir
1 cup sugar
2 tablespoons LuLu Fig Cherry & Balsamic Jam
about 15 fresh mint leaves
1 quart vanilla ice cream

Preparation: In a large bowl, combine cherry halves with lemon juice and set aside.

Heat wine in a large saucepot over medium heat and simmer until reduced by half; do not boil. Stir in sugar, 1 cup water, LuLu Fig Cherry & Balsamic Jam and reserved cherries, remove from heat and set aside.

Chiffonade mint leaves by slicing them into very thin strips; do not chop mint leaves.

To assemble: spoon cherry sauce into martini glasses or small bowls and top each with a scoop of vanilla ice cream. Sprinkle with mint chiffonade and serve.

Note: Just as asparagus heralds the arrival of spring, the appearance of
              cherries in markets means that summer is approaching. Fresh cherries
              are generally available between June and August. We prefer using
              Bing cherries in this recipe, but any sweet variety, such as Royal Ann or
              Lambert, will do.

Other LuLu   If LuLu Fig Cherry & Balsamic Jam is not available, substitute another
Products: LuLu Jam.

Balsamic Fruit Salad
with Lavender Honey Whipped Cream
6 to 8 servings

Featuring: **LuLu Fig & Meyer Lemon Balsamic Vinegar**
LuLu Essence of Lavender Honey

Ingredients: 2 pounds assorted fruit such as berries, stone fruit and melons
2 tablespoons LuLu Fig & Meyer Lemon Balsamic Vinegar
4 tablespoons LuLu Essence of Lavender Honey
1 cup heavy whipping cream
coarsely chopped toasted hazelnuts for garnish if desired
fresh mint sprigs for garnish if desired

Preparation: Rinse berries. Cut stone fruit in half, remove pits, and cut into quarters. Peel melons, remove seeds, and cut into large cubes about the same size as cut stone fruit. In a large bowl, toss fruit with LuLu Fig & Meyer Lemon Balsamic Vinegar and set aside.

In a medium bowl, stir 2 tablespoons LuLu Essence of Lavender Honey into cream and then beat into whipped cream.

To serve: spoon fruit salad into individual bowls and sprinkle with hazelnuts if desired. Top fruit with a dollop of lavender honey whipped cream and a drizzle of remaining LuLu Essence of Lavender Honey. Garnish with mint sprigs if desired.

Note:	*This versatile recipe can be prepared any time of the year with whatever fresh fruit is available. An alternative preparation is to toss cut stone fruit with 1 tablespoon extra virgin olive oil, grill fruit for a few minutes over high heat, toss grilled fruit with LuLu Fig & Meyer Lemon Balsamic Vinegar, and proceed with serving directions.*
Other LuLu Products:	*If LuLu Fig & Meyer Lemon Balsamic Vinegar is not available, substitute another LuLu Balsamic Vinegar.*

Meyer Lemon and Rosemary Pound Cake

6 to 8 servings

Featuring: **LuLu Meyer Lemon Curd**

Ingredients:
1-1/2 cups all-purpose flour
1/2 teaspoon salt
1 teaspoon baking powder
6-1/2 ounces (1 stick plus 5 tablespoons) unsalted butter
   at room temperature
3/4 cup plus 2 tablespoons sugar
4 eggs
2 tablespoons extra virgin olive oil
2 tablespoons chopped fresh rosemary
1/3 cup LuLu Meyer Lemon Curd, plus more for serving

Preparation:
Preheat oven to 350°.

Butter and flour a loaf pan.

In a medium bowl, sift together flour, salt and baking powder and set aside. In an electric mixer fitted with the paddle attachment, beat together butter and sugar at high speed until light and fluffy. Reduce mixer speed to medium and add eggs one at a time, blending thoroughly after each addition. Add olive oil, then add LuLu Meyer Lemon Curd. Add flour mixture in batches and continue mixing for 2 to 3 minutes until flour is just blended into batter.

Pour batter into prepared loaf pan and bake for about 1 hour; cake is done when a toothpick inserted into the center comes out "clean" without batter or many crumbs on it.

Cool cake in loaf pan on a wire rack.

To serve: when cake has cooled, remove it from loaf pan and cut into 3/4-inch thick slices. Serve with additional LuLu Meyer Lemon Curd to dollop onto cake slices.

Note: We recommend baking this cake the day before you plan to serve it to give the flavors time to develop. The fresh rosemary helps to balance the acidity of the lemon and sweetness of the sugar, but it can be omitted if desired.

Fig and Raspberry Tart

8 servings

Featuring:	**LuLu Fig Strawberry & Balsamic Jam** **LuLu Essence of Orange Blossom Honey**

Ingredients:
- 12 ounces (3 sticks) unsalted butter
- 1/2 cup plus 1 tablespoon sugar
- 3 eggs
- 3 cups pastry flour
- 6 ounces almond paste
- 3 tablespoons all-purpose flour
- 1/2 cup LuLu Fig Strawberry & Balsamic Jam
- 2 pints fresh figs, stemmed and cut into quarters
- 1 pint fresh raspberries
- 1/4 cup LuLu Essence of Orange Blossom Honey
- 1/2 cup sliced almonds, toasted

Preparation:

Divide butter: remove 6 tablespoons butter from refrigerator and let it soften to room temperature.

Prepare tart dough: in an electric mixer fitted with the paddle attachment, beat cold butter with 1/2 cup sugar at medium speed until smooth. Add 1 egg, then add pastry flour and continue mixing for 2 to 3 minutes until dough just holds together. Gather dough into a ball and flatten into a 1-inch thick disk. Wrap in plastic wrap and refrigerate.

Prepare frangipane: in an electric mixer beat almond paste, softened butter and remaining sugar at high speed until light and fluffy. Add all-purpose flour and mix at medium speed for 2 to 3 minutes until blended. Add remaining eggs, one at a time, blending thoroughly after each addition. Spoon frangipane into an airtight container, cover and refrigerate.

Remove tart dough from refrigerator and roll it out on a lightly floured surface to a 1/8-inch thickness. Press dough into a 10-inch tart pan and trim edges with a paring knife. Using an offset metal spatula, evenly spread a 1/2-inch layer of frangipane into tart shell. Refrigerate for 20 minutes.

continued

Preheat oven to 350°.

Remove tart pan from refrigerator and place onto a large baking sheet. Bake for 15 to 20 minutes until both tart shell and frangipane are golden brown. Remove from oven and cool on a wire rack.

When tart has cooled, spread LuLu Fig Strawberry & Balsamic Jam over the frangipane. Arrange figs in a spiral on top of the jam, working inward from the edge, then arrange raspberries on top of figs. In a small bowl, combine 2 tablespoons warm water with LuLu Essence of Orange Blossom Honey and brush mixture over figs and raspberries. Sprinkle with almonds and serve.

Apple Crostada with Meyer Lemon Marmalade
8 servings

Featuring: **LuLu Meyer Lemon Marmalade**
LuLu Essence of Lavender Honey

Ingredients: 6 large Granny Smith apples
1 sheet (1/2 of a 17-1/4 ounce package) frozen puff pastry
4 tablespoons LuLu Meyer Lemon Marmalade
4 tablespoons LuLu Essence of Lavender Honey
1 cup heavy whipping cream

Preparation: Preheat oven to 300°.

Core and peel apples, but do not cut into pieces. Place apples on a baking sheet and roast them for 45 to 50 minutes until slightly soft and lightly browned. Remove apples from oven and allow them to cool.

While apples are baking thaw the puff pastry sheet. Roll out puff pastry to a 1/8-inch thickness and trim into a circle 13 inches in diameter. Fold in the edges to make a 12-inch round and place dough flat into the freezer to chill.

Increase oven temperature to 400°

Cut cooled apples in half and then slice each half into 1/8-inch wedges.

Remove dough from freezer and place onto a baking sheet. Spread 3 tablespoons LuLu Meyer Lemon Marmalade across the dough, leaving a 1-inch border. Arrange apple slices in a fan on top of the marmalade and brush with remaining marmalade. Place in oven and bake for 15 to 18 minutes until golden brown. Remove from oven and allow crostada to cool.

Meanwhile stir 2 tablespoons LuLu Essence of Lavender Honey into cream and then beat into whipped cream. Set aside.

To serve: cut crostada into 8 slices. Serve each slice topped with a dollop of lavender honey whipped cream and a drizzle of remaining LuLu Essence of Lavender Honey. Serve warm or at room temperature.

Note: Granny Smith apples are green-skinned, slightly tart, and perfect for this recipe because they hold their shape and do not become mushy during the 2-step baking process. You can substitute any firm apple if Granny Smiths are not available.

Other LuLu
Products: If LuLu Meyer Lemon Marmalade is not available, substitute another LuLu Marmalade.

Pumpkin Amaretti Tart
with Orange Honey Whipped Cream

8 servings

Featuring: **LuLu Essence of Orange Blossom Honey**

Ingredients:
3 cups all-purpose flour, chilled
1 teaspoon salt
12 ounces (3 sticks) unsalted butter, cut into tablespoons and chilled
2/3 cup ice water
1 sugar pie pumpkin, about 2 pounds
1 jar LuLu Essence of Orange Blossom Honey
1 cup amaretti (Italian almond macaroons) cookie crumbs
2 tablespoons sugar
1 cup heavy whipping cream

Preparation:
Prepare tart dough: in a large bowl, stir together flour and salt. Using a pastry blender or fork, cut 18 tablespoons of the chilled butter into flour until mixture looks crumbly and only tiny pieces of butter are visible. Mix in ice water, a few drops at a time, until dough begins to hold together; you may not need to use all of the water. Gather dough into a ball, wrap in plastic wrap and refrigerate for at least 3 hours.

Preheat oven to 400°.

Cut pumpkin into wedges, remove seeds and roast pumpkin for 30 to 40 minutes until fork-tender. Remove from oven and allow to cool. Peel wedges, pass through a food mill or mash by hand, and set aside.

Set aside 2 tablespoons LuLu Essence of Orange Blossom Honey. In a small saucepot, heat remaining honey and butter over medium heat for 3 to 5 minutes until light brown. In a large bowl combine pumpkin and amaretti crumbs, then stir in honey mixture. Set aside to cool.

Preheat oven to 425°.

Remove dough from refrigerator and cut into two pieces, one slightly larger than the other. Roll both pieces out on a lightly floured surface into circles with a 1/8-inch thickness.

continued

Spread pumpkin mixture across the smaller pastry circle, leaving a 1-1/2-inch border. Fold border up around filling and brush outside edge lightly with water. Lay larger disc over tart and tuck around outside of bottom crust, cutting away any excess dough. Sprinkle top with sugar and cut 3 steam vents into it with a sharp knife. Place on cookie sheet and bake for 15 to 20 minutes until crust is golden brown. Remove from oven and cool on a wire rack.

In a medium bowl, stir remaining honey into cream and then beat into whipped cream.

To serve: slice tart into wedges, top each with a dollop of orange honey whipped cream and serve.

Meyer Lemon and Berry Tarts

4 servings

Featuring: **LuLu Meyer Lemon Curd**

Ingredients: 4 pastry shells, about 4 inches in diameter
1 jar LuLu Meyer Lemon Curd
1/2 cup fresh strawberries, stemmed and cut into quarters
1/2 cup fresh blackberries
fresh mint sprigs for garnish

Preparation: Bake pastry shells unfilled according to package directions and cool on a wire rack.

To assemble tarts: fill cooled pastry shells most of the way up the sides with LuLu Meyer Lemon Curd. Decoratively arrange berries on top of curd. Garnish with mint sprigs and serve.

Note: *Although you can prepare your own pastry dough, it is more convenient to purchase frozen or refrigerated pastry shells, or even pre-baked ones. You can use any type of berry to top the tarts, and even substitute slices or wedges of fruit, such as kiwis or plums.*

Chocolate Caramel Brownies

24 brownies

Featuring: **LuLu Fig Cherry & Balsamic Jam**

Ingredients:
5 tablespoons LuLu Fig Cherry & Balsamic Jam
1/3 cup plus 1/2 cup heavy whipping cream
3 cups sugar
1-1/2 teaspoons corn syrup
9-1/2 ounces (2 sticks plus 3 tablespoons) unsalted butter
1-3/4 pounds semisweet chocolate, chopped
2-1/2 cups all-purpose flour
1/2 teaspoon baking soda
1/4 teaspoon baking powder
1/4 teaspoon salt
6 eggs
2 tablespoons vanilla extract

Preparation:
Preheat oven to 325°.

Butter a large baking sheet and line with parchment paper.

Prepare caramel: in a small bowl, blend LuLu Fig Cherry & Balsamic Jam with 1/3 cup cream. In a medium saucepot, heat 1/2 cup sugar and corn syrup over high heat and boil for 3 to 5 minutes until medium brown. Remove from heat and whisk in jam mixture, then 1 tablespoon butter, and set aside.

Prepare brownie batter: in a double-boiler, melt 1 pound chocolate with remaining butter and remaining cream. Stir to combine. Remove from heat and set aside to cool.

In a medium bowl, sift together flour, baking soda, baking powder and salt. In an electric mixer fitted with the whisk attachment, beat together remaining sugar with eggs and vanilla at medium speed until smooth. Temper the egg mixture by whisking 1 tablespoon of the chocolate mixture into it. Whisk in remaining chocolate mixture, then add flour mixture and continue whisking for 2 to 3 minutes until just blended together.

continued

Using a spatula, fold half of the remaining chopped chocolate into batter. Pour batter into prepared baking sheet, top with remaining chocolate and drizzle with 3/4 cup caramel. Bake for 30 to 35 minutes until brownies pull away from edges of baking sheet. Remove from oven and cool in pan on a wire rack. Cut into 24 pieces and serve.

Note: *If there is any leftover caramel sauce, cover and refrigerate it until ready to use. To serve, gently warm in a bain marie and drizzle over ice cream, pound cake slices or apple pie.*

Other LuLu
Products: *If LuLu Fig Cherry & Balsamic Jam is not available, substitute another LuLu Jam.*

Tangerine Rhubarb Tuile Cookies

8 servings

Featuring: **LuLu Tangerine & Rhubarb Marmalade**

Ingredients:
1-1/2 cups confectioners' (powdered) sugar
6 egg whites
1-1/3 cups all-purpose flour
4 ounces (1 stick) unsalted butter at room temperature
3 tablespoons LuLu Tangerine & Rhubarb Marmalade
8 ounces semisweet chocolate, chopped

Preparation:
In an electric mixer fitted with the whisk attachment, whisk together sugar and egg whites at high speed until just combined. Add flour and continue whisking until batter is smooth. Add half of the butter and continue whisking until it is blended into batter, then blend in remaining butter. Whisk in LuLu Tangerine & Rhubarb Marmalade until just combined. Remove bowl from mixer, cover with plastic wrap and refrigerate for at least 2 hours.

Preheat oven to 300°.

Line a baking sheet with a silicone baking liner or parchment paper.

Using a 2- by 3-inch plastic stencil (or make your own by cutting a 2- by 3-inch rectangle into the lid of a disposable plastic food container), spread a thin layer of batter through stencil onto prepared baking sheet. Keeping rectangles 1-inch apart, repeat with stencil and remaining batter. (Bake in batches using additional lined baking sheets if necessary.) Bake cookies for 4 to 5 minutes until lightly browned at edges.

Remove from oven and immediately shape each cookie by peeling it from the baking sheet with a metal spatula and rolling it around a pencil. Cool rolled cookies on a wire rack.

Once cookies have cooled, melt chocolate in a microwave at high heat for 30 seconds. Stir and return chocolate to microwave for 30 more seconds. Repeat if necessary until chocolate has completely melted; do not overcook.

continued

Line a clean baking sheet with parchment paper. Dip each cookie halfway into melted chocolate and place on parchment paper. Refrigerate for 5 minutes to set chocolate.

To serve: remove cookies from refrigerator and allow them to warm to room temperature. Arrange on a platter and serve.

Note: *The key to success with tuile cookies is to work quickly while shaping them. Make sure to roll cookies while they are still warm and pliable; they will become brittle within minutes as they cool. For beginners, start with a batch of 6 cookies per baking sheet until you feel confident enough to work faster.*

Orange Honey Shortbread Cookie Sandwiches with Fig and Strawberry Jam

36 cookies

Featuring:
LuLu Essence of Orange Blossom Honey
LuLu Fig Strawberry & Balsamic Jam

Ingredients:
2-1/2 cups all-purpose flour
1/2 cup cornstarch
1 teaspoon salt
12 ounces (3 sticks) unsalted butter at room temperature
1 cup confectioners' (powdered) sugar plus more for garnish if desired
2 tablespoons LuLu Essence of Orange Blossom Honey
1 jar LuLu Fig Strawberry & Balsamic Jam

Preparation:
Preheat oven to 300°.

In a medium bowl, stir together flour, cornstarch and salt. In an electric mixer fitted with the paddle attachment, beat together butter, sugar, and LuLu Essence of Orange Blossom Honey at high speed until light and fluffy. Add flour mixture and continue mixing for 2 to 3 minutes until dough just holds together.

Gather dough into a ball and roll it out on a floured surface into a 1/4-inch thick rectangle. Trim edges to make the sides of the rectangle straight. Cut dough in the long direction into 1-inch wide strips, then cut across dough into 2-inch wide strips to yield 1- by 2-inch rectangles.

Line a baking sheet with parchment paper. Place cookies in a single layer on baking sheet. (Bake in batches using additional lined baking sheets if necessary.) Bake for 8 to 10 minutes, until edges are lightly browned.

Remove baking sheet from oven and place onto a wire rack to cool for 3 minutes. Remove individual cookies from sheet with a metal spatula and place onto wire rack to continue cooling.

continued

To assemble cookies: spread 1 teaspoon LuLu Fig Strawberry & Balsamic Jam onto one cookie, top with a second cookie and gently press together to form a sandwich. Repeat with remaining cookies. Sprinkle cookies with additional confectioners' sugar if desired and serve.

Note: *Traditionally, shortbread cookies were associated with Christmas festivities, but nowadays children and adults alike enjoy this butter-rich cookie all year long. These cookies can be stored for up to 5 days in a covered, airtight container.*

Other LuLu   *If LuLu Fig Strawberry & Balsamic Jam is not available, substitute another*
Products: *LuLu Jam.*

LuLu Locations

Restaurant LuLu Gourmet Products are available at specialty food retailers nationwide and around the world, or you can contact us directly at the following address:

Restaurant LuLu Gourmet Products
1245 Folsom St.
San Francisco, CA 94103
888-693-5800
fax: 415-255-8668
email: customerservice@restaurantlulu.com
www.restaurantlulu.com

You can also find our products at any one of our restaurants:

Restaurant LuLu
816 Folsom St.
San Francisco, CA 94107
415-495-5775

Restaurant LuLu at Mammoth
1111 Forest Trail, Unit 201
Mammoth Lakes, CA 93546
760-924-8781

Zibibbo
430 Kipling St.
Palo Alto, CA 94301
650-328-6722

Azie
826 Folsom St.
San Francisco, CA 94107
415-538-0918

and at any one of our gourmet delicatessens:

LuLu Petite San Francisco
1 Ferry Building, Shop # 19
San Francisco, CA 94111
415-362-7019

LuLu Petite Palo Alto
430 Kipling St.
(entrance on Waverly)
Palo Alto, CA 94301
650-328-6722

LuLu Petite University Circle
1950 University Ave., Ste. 100
East Palo Alto, CA 94303
650-329-8668

LuLu Petite Mammoth Lakes
1111 Forest Trail, Unit 201
Mammoth Lakes, CA 93546
760-924-8781

Recipe Index by LuLu Product

Blue type indicates LuLu Product names

Recipe Index